ENDORSE[

This journey of a pastor, his family they changed a city envisioned, em[ ]quipped by the **Holy Spirit.** It is a story of how they have and are bringing and advancing the kingdom in a city that was broken, desolate and without hope. It is a unique testimony of what God can do and what is possible beyond their (our) wildest dreams.

The book describes their Holy Spirit directed journey from leaving a leading successful church in a large city to establishing a kingdom beachhead in a city desperate for a way out. It is a story of sacrifice, obedience to direct leading of the Holy Spirit and perseverance under the most trying of circumstances. It is a testimony of Gods faithfulness, love and commission to disciple a nation starting with a city.

The story of Brantford is proof positive that the kingdom of Jesus can be advanced and that injustice and unrighteousness can be reduced and eliminated resulting in peace and joy transforming a city in the process. Feeding hungry children in school, or serving burgers on the street during the wee hours of the morning has given Brian and his team credibility in business, government, and education who then have joined him in going further and doing more than he ever imagined. Public baptisms in city square, winter carnivals, and movie nights, live nativity scenes, are just the visible signs of the deeper transformation that is going on in Brantford. The economy is prospering, vacant downtown storefronts have disappeared, a university is flourishing. City hall is partnering with provincial, and federal politicians of different stripes. The media is writing monthly stories about what is happening. The churches are collaborating with government and businesses providing innovative solutions to address issues of poverty, at all levels in the community. The transformation that is happening is measurable, sustainable and real. Extraordinary miracles are happening at every level throughout Brantford.

Brian outlines the kingdom principles and Holy Spirit inspired strategies that are evident in scripture that can be used and applied in every city large or small across this great nation of Canada and beyond.

This book is a "must read" for everyone who has a stirring in their heart to make things better in their family, their street, their job, their community, their city, their nation. What is possible and has happened in Brantford is possible across this nation. Brian it has been a pleasure and joy to journey with you, learn from you and celebrate with you as to what God is doing in your town.

Derk Maat
Chair/CEO Transformation Canada
Toronto, Canada

Reading this book was like hearing Brian talk enthusiastically and excitedly about his congregation, Freedom House; about the unity of ONEchurch; about the innovative Community Task Force; and the growing crowd of people who have joined in serving the city. Brantford started reflecting more and more of the goodness, peace and joy that are God's great dream for all of our cities. Brian is a Spiritual Father to the movement of Brantford's being transformed into a city on a hill, one that shines light into darkness and provides light for all who come near. Listen! You too can hear the clear word of their testimony as you read this book. It's a powerful word, a powerful overcoming testimony and it shines with light.

Annita Maat
Transformation Canada
Toronto, Canada

A story of big dreams, **huge risk and hard work.** The old-time hymn "Trust and Obey" kept ringing in my mind, repeating as the core message colouring Brian's book of how the power of faith has driven the transformation of our city. The unconventional Freedom House leadership approach has resulted in God's blessing to all parts of the community, while positively changing and saving individual lives along the way. The message is clear; believe, go for it, and never give up! Trust and Obey.

Phil McColeman, MP
Brantford/Brant, Canada

I myself have dreamt of taking cities for Jesus. I've read books about it, but always by people who have never actually taken one. Of course, it has happened in the past, by Jesus and the early church; in the Book of Acts and beyond. But in our day?... But, Brian Beattie is a passionate, prayerful, and determined follower of Jesus who is well on his way to taking his beloved Brantford, Ontario.

If you have a heart for community transformation, you will be greatly encouraged by Brian's amazing ongoing story.

John Arnott
Catch the Fire & Partners in Harvest, Toronto
Toronto, Canada

"This is a book that had to be written. There is a 20-minute video documentary of the story that in no way explains the magnitude of what is happening in the city of Brantford. What Dr. Brian Beattie manages to do in this book is to be authentic, inspiring and share the dirt of what took much longer to happen then he thought. This is a 101 book on city transformation. It's theologically sound, faith inspiring and pragmatic to the point; you can do it in your town or city.

Here you have a journey of 15 years articulated in a way that is insightful and practical. When you read this, get ready, as you will want to be a part of the team that will transform your community."

Ian Green
"Working Towards Global Transformation."
Bedworth, UK
www.iangreen.org

"Finally! I have observed much of the Brantford, City of God process for the entirety of the incredible journey. I have heard and witnessed many of these stories first hand, told and re-told many of the stories myself. These accounts are too epic NOT to be told. What Brian and his team have done is nothing short of God-inspired, faithful, consistent, resilient efforts to enact God's word with practical, loving excellence, arguably more effectively than anyone I have ever seen. The principles behind the stories are the game-changing concepts that every Christian should be living out today. I am thrilled to finally see the story in print. Be careful. Adherence to these ideas will definitely change your world."

Rev. D. Mark Griffin
Speaker, Author
Brantford, Canada
www.markgriffin.ca

When I was 20 years old, I met Brian Beattie and my life has never been the same. We shared a like passion for city transformation and seeing God's Church become fully alive. He allowed me, as a young man, to come with him on the journey that this book details; making me the man I am today. Brian's visionary leadership and fearless devotion to hearing, and obeying God's heart for cities makes him a voice to pay close attention to. This book is a very important one as it will serve as inspiration and is filled with applicable, powerful, ideas that can change your city in tangible ways.

Dave Carrol *A.K.A. "Captain Kindness"*
Freedom House Community Pastor
Brantford, Canada

The stories are outrageous, but the impact is clear! To read some of these stories one might be tempted to believe that they are simply exaggerated to make a point. However, as one who has experienced them and seen the aftermath, I can attest that these stories are real, if not understated. The people are real. The impact is tangible, and the transformation is ongoing. Under Brian's leadership I have grown to understand that each of us has a role to play in transformation. I hope you see yours more clearly as you read our story.

Nicolette Straza

Freedom House Discipleship/Leadership Pastor
Brantford, Canada

A fantastic read! Much more so because I know and love many of the leaders mentioned in this book. I love the pioneering, 'all in' passion and practice that I see in Brian and his team. There are many theorists within the Transformation movement. This book tells the story of a church and team that bridges the gap from theory to practice every day as they seek to see their city transformed. This book will make your heart beat a bit faster as God stretches your faith and vision to believe that you can be a part of seeing your city transformed in remarkable ways too!

Tim Schindel
Victoria, Canada
www.leadinginfluence.com

Many people talk about transformation, some have experienced it, but relatively few have played a leading role in making it a reality. For the past five years I have watched Brian Beattie lead in the transformation of Brantford, but this was only possible after he experienced transformation in his heart. This book gives us a personal, front-row seat to that process from its start to the present day, with a watchful anticipation of what Brantford is becoming as the City of God. My prayer is that this story will become a catalyst for transformational conversations around the globe.

Rev. Brian A. Mullins
Regional Advisor World Vision Canada
Cambridge, Canada

"Brian Beattie and his transformation cohorts at Freedom House are the epitome of "ordinary people doing extraordinary deeds" to see their city and nation transformed. Brian's nitty-gritty, wysiwyg, (what you see is what you get) and humourous delivery will jerk you into his account of their journey over and over again. Get ready to be ambushed by God into believing that your city, like theirs, can become God's city!"

Dave Thompson
Sr. Vice President
Harvest Evangelism/Transform Our World
San José, USA
www.transformourworld.org

I have been to Brantford, and to Freedom House on multiple occasions. I have wept as people who were unknown to Freedom House showed up at the Baptism in Harmony Square and asked, "What must I do to get baptized?" I also stood alongside Captain Kindness at the one-dollar car wash, when a lady drove in and exclaimed, "Wow, one dollar is a pretty low price for a car wash!" The driver was even more astonished when Captain Kindness blessed her with one dollar for the privilege of washing her car. Yes, Brantford is on its way to becoming the kindest city in Canada! I enthusiastically endorse this book by Pastor Brian Beattie. Study these principles and implement them in your own city.

Rick Heeren

Author of the following books; The Elk River Story, Thank God It's Monday, The Threshing Floor and Marketplace Miracles
Transform Our World
Minneapolis, USA

So inspiring to know how God is on the move transforming a "ghost and depressed city" to a live and vibrant city by applying the simple but powerful principle of "hear God and obey." Brian with his characteristically spontaneous and inspirational eloquence describes a true and down to earth faith journey by doing extraordinary deeds, being an ordinary believer. As you read "City of God" you are going to be inspired and motivated to follow such amazing concepts and principals as: "hear God and obey", "the B.E.S.T life", "show the love of God in a practical way", "Superhero in Me, "I really like your baby", "wwckd?", "Flippin' Fridays", "the power of the burger", "ONEchurch", "cultural architects", "low J-count or high J-count", "it will only be hard if you expect ease", this is a good one: "Polipneumaclimatologist". And all of this is biblically based with one single purpose in mind: To glorify Jesus!

Poncho Murguia
Transform Our World,
Juarez, Mexico

Warning: this book can seriously change your life! It is very rare to read something that doesn't just tell a true story, but inspires and challenges you to do something about the city where you live. In this book, Brian Beattie shares the story of how he, with his wife Sharlyss, discovered how to restore hope to a city that had no hope. In fact, they had even given up on Brantford themselves until God intervened. As Brian shares their journey, beginning with the all-important starting point of Transformation (God revealing His heart for the city to them) the reader is taken on a journey of discovery of how to minister God's love to the whole community.

Brian's writing style is like his preaching, matter of fact teaching with a slice of dry humor that leaves you feeling both blessed and challenged at the same time. You will be taken on a journey of the author's personal transformation that has led, and is still leading many others to bring change to their city and beyond to their nation. It is not really possible for this book to have an end, because the story is continuing, transformation is still going on in Brantford... and so my heartfelt endorsement for you to read it is this... the next chapter of the story should be written by YOU!

Brian Burton
Senior Pastor, Phuket Christian Centre
Transform Our World
Phuket, Thailand

The Kindness of God leads to City Transformation: "Listen to God and obey" is the prescription Pastor Brian Beattie gives us to totally transform a city. To do intentional acts of kindness and blessings wins the hearts of not only the poor, but also politicians and those of economic prowess alike. This book, "City of God" is masterful and clear on the power of

City of God

Copyright ©2019 Brian Beattie

Published by Freedom House Publishing

www.freedomhouse.ca

1 Market Street, Suite 103, Brantford, Ontario N3T 6C8, Canada, 226-401-3626

This title is available from publisher only.

Cover & Layout by Nicolette Straza, Sharlyss & Brian Beattie.

All scripture quotations, unless otherwise indicated, are taken from the Holy Bible, *New International Version*® NIV®. Copyright © 1973, 1978, 1984, 2011 by Biblica, Inc.™ Used by permission of Zondervan. All rights reserved worldwide. www.zondervan.com. The "NIV" and "New International Version" are trademarks registered in the United States Patent and Trademark Office by Biblica, Inc.™

All rights reserved. No portion of this book may be reproduced, store in a retrieval system, or transmitted in any form or by any means – electronic, mechanical, photocopy, record, or any other – except for brief quotation in printed reviews, without the prior permission of the publisher.

❧ Created with Vellum

CITY of GOD

Transformed People, Transforming Cities

Brian Beattie Ph.D.

DEDICATION

※

This book is dedicated to My Family:

Sharlyss - The incomparable one. I am convinced that when we get to Heaven I will find out that most of what transpired in our lives was because of your prayers.

Renyck - The victorious one

Brayden - The adventurous one

Vanessa - The gracious one

THANKS

Our Transform Our World Family who constantly remind us to be humble and hungry. You *REALLY* are "ordinary people doing extraordinary deeds."

Our Freedom House Family who constantly and consistently serve as a source of strength and encouragement. You exemplify "loving God, loving others, and loving extravagantly."

Sharlyss Beattie your meticulous skills are very much appreciated.

Nicolette Straza your contributions and hard work made this possible.

ABOUT THE AUTHOR

Brian Beattie Ph.D.

Brian is a husband, father, speaker, writer and visionary leader. He has been described as passionate, compassionate, courageous, direct and tenacious.

He is presently the Lead Pastor of *Freedom House* in Brantford, Ontario; the President of Freedom Training Centre and on both the National and International Teams of *Transform Our World*.

Brian is also the founder and owner of *Leadership by Design*, a consulting company working with individuals and groups to enhance personality, passion and performance.

 facebook.com/brian.beattie.9

CONTENTS

Foreword by Dr. Ed Silvoso	xxi
Introduction	xxv
1. Brantford - The City We Used to Drive Around.	1
2. The Vision for Cities	5
3. Three Strikes and You're…?	15
4. The City of God	21
5. Can You Name the City You Are Fighting for?	29
6. Hear God and Obey	35
7. Freedom House - A Ministry Centre Where Church Happens	47
8. The Kindest City in Canada	59
9. ONEchurch - Participating in the Transformation of the City	75
10. The Gospel of the Kingdom	85
11. The Culture of the Kingdom	101
12. The Myth of Church and State Separation	107
13. Other City Champions	119
14. A Tale of Two Cities	129
15. Making Your City, the City of God	137
Notes	141
APPENDIX	145
How to Transform a City	147
Freedom Encounter	153
Superhero in Me	155
The KINDNESS PROJECT	157
Epilogue	159

FOREWARD BY DR. ED SILVOSO

God loves cities. He also loves nations because they make up the world for which He gave His only begotten Son. His ultimate desire is eloquently presented in Revelation 21:24-27 – a parade of nations that have been saved. And the key for this is seeing cities transformed since nations are made up of a constellation of cities.

No one in Christendom doubts that God wants to see cities transformed, but not everybody knows of cities that are currently undergoing transformation. Well, wait no more! Brian and Sharlyss Beattie have been used by God, along with their team of world changers at Freedom House in Brantford, Ontario, Canada, to demonstrate that cities can and must be transformed. This is what this book, *City of God*, is all about. It is not just another book written by a theoretician. On the contrary, Brian writes in a most inspiring way. He has been gifted with an anointed prose that brilliantly combines anecdotes and contemporary examples with biblical principles.

The wisdom and the testimonies that Brian so masterfully presents in this book, along with the biblical principles, will inspire and empower you to believe that your city can be transformed too. And more important yet, that God wants to use you to do it. We all know that without God we can't accomplish anything, but what Brian reminds us of is that without *us*

God won't do it. This is the intriguing mystery of transformation, that God almighty has chosen us to be co-laborers with Christ to change the world.

In the Transform Our World movement that my wife and I have the privilege of leading, Brantford, Ontario, is a prime example of why and how cities can and must be transformed. As you begin to read, be aware that you may not be able to put this book down until you get to the last page. And when you do, it is my fervent prayer that you will apply the principles so that your city can also experience transformation.

Dr. Ed Silvoso
President and Founder, Transform Our World
Author, *Anointed for Business* and *Ekklesia*

CITY OF GOD

Transformed People, Transforming Cities

BRIAN BEATTIE, PH.D.

INTRODUCTION

"*Mr. Speaker, eight years ago, Freedom House, a church and Ministry Centre in Brantford began on a mission called the Kindness Project to see if a city could be transformed 'by good into good' using simple, but strategic acts of kindness.*

In these eight years, among other things, roughly 20,000 hamburgers have been given away; a free Winter Carnival: Frosty Fest is hosted; a school curriculum is in the works; Affordable Housing has been built providing for those in need; a local Superhero, Captain Kindness has emerged and taken control of the city...

The Kindness Project seeks to uncover the untapped level of synergy in our community as a collective commitment to serving each other, it's people helping people with what we all have in our hands to give. Mr. Speaker, we hope, together, to make Brantford known as the KINDEST CITY IN CANADA".

These were the words our local Member of Parliament, Phil McColeman used in our nation's capital, speaking about what had been accomplished in our city to that point.

How do I know our city is being transformed?

Well, we see tangible evidence of it everywhere, in every sphere of our city. I'll tell many of the stories throughout this book of how the church in the city is being invited to many of the seats of influence to bring positive, consistent transformation. But, one conversation stands out to me as significant evidence to the transformation of our city.

INTRODUCTION

Many of the key leaders in our city were gathering at Phil McColeman's house that night to discuss a major event which his team would be running in a few days. I was chairing the event and the evening's meeting.

As I walked into the meeting, I was seriously wondering if years of relationship building and service to the community may have already been erased, by our bold stand for Christ the previous weekend. But, I walked out of the meeting, marveling at the goodness and glory of God. I watched in amazement as God orchestrated the convergence of many of the key leaders of our city together in one place, spun the discussion away from the potential challenge, into an engaging and genuine dialogue about God and His designs on our city (with ongoing, positive impact to this very day).

While it was both shocking and exhilarating at the same time, I have seen God repeat this same type of scenario over and over again, as He reveals His great love and mercy to all who will listen.

There's no mystery to city transformation. Get outside of the church - love & serve people. *If you want to have influence, you have to have involvement.*

We didn't know what to expect when we moved to Brantford and started Freedom House. Had we known how challenging it was going to be – we may not have come. Had we known how amazing it was going to be – we may have come earlier.

But, we now know, what once was a dream is becoming a reality – Brantford is becoming the *City of God.*

For the record, we don't claim that our city is transformed. The truth is, there are still many issues that we are working on; still areas that we are actively and intentionally bringing the kingdom of God to with His righteousness, peace and joy.

However, we have come a long, long way from having the "worst downtown in Canada" and no one could argue that Brantford now has one of the most thriving, alive downtowns anywhere. Brantford is a city, where business, education, government and the *Ekklesia* are working together to create a transformation that is being recognized nationally and internationally.

The connections and friendships that we now have both locally and globally are far beyond anything we could have imagined. Specifically, our connection and partnership with the Transform Our World Network founded by Dr. Ed Silvoso which continues to be a source of inspiration and encouragement. What was once admiration from a distance has become close personal friendships and mutual encouragement within this group that we have come to love as family.

In the winter of 2000, several churches had come together for a worship evening. One of the ladies from our church was given a very specific vision that became a rallying cry even up to the present day.

"What did you see Marie?"

"I saw the sign on the highway change from *Brantford – a Grand Experience*, to *Brantford - City of God*."

This is our story...

1

BRANTFORD - THE CITY WE USED TO DRIVE AROUND.

"WE ARE NEVER GOING BACK TO THAT CITY AS LONG AS I LIVE!" Those were the first words that my wife spoke when she got home that night.

"What happened, dear?" were my carefully selected words.

For the next 30 minutes, I heard all about how a wonderful girl's night out at the mall had ended. My wife Sharlyss and her friend Laura, had enjoyed a great evening of shopping and a movie. But, on the way to their car to drive home, they were approached and accosted by a couple of what she described as *"that city's most interesting individuals."*

Over the next few days I heard the same story told repeatedly with various tones and adjectives describing both the city, and the men who made the ladies visit to *that city* anything but pleasant.

So, being the good husband that I am, I honoured my wife's request and we never went back to that city. In fact, we would intentionally drive *around* that city. We would drive around it go to numerous other cities for shopping, nights out and entertainment. My wife had given very clear instructions that we were *never* to visit *that city* again. And since I had previously learned the adage, "Happy Wife, Happy Life", for almost a decade we avoided *that city*.

"THAT CITY" was Brantford.

Ironically, Brantford is the place God called us to move to years later, when He asked us if we could believe that a city could be transformed. Today our church is in the very mall where she and her friend had been accosted. It is from here that we have been honoured to be part of the transformation of our city. Our city is being transformed. Lives are being transformed. Schools, businesses and neighbourhoods are seeing remarkable proof of the transforming power of the gospel of the Kingdom. We have seen real, tangible evidence of the Kingdom of God coming to our city just like it is in heaven.

And, it's not just in our city. All over the world the spirit of God is moving. He is moving the hearts of men and women in both the church and the marketplace to partner with His plan for their cities.

Do you believe that God has a plan for your city? If God did have a plan, what kind of plan would it be?

Well, we know it would be a good plan. It would be a plan full of hope. It would be a plan of peace and prosperity.

How do we know this?

Jeremiah 29:11 For I know the plans I have for you," declares the LORD, "plans to prosper you and not to harm you, plans to give you hope and a future.

We love this verse, don't we? We quote it often; we write songs about it. We put it on our fridges.

But do we believe it?

You probably wouldn't be holding this book in your hand if you didn't have hope that God could change a city. God does have a plan for you and your city and He is anxiously waiting to partner with you to see the people and systems of your city transformed by His Kingdom.

Our story has been told on every continent on the globe and has always provided proof that God will use anyone and anything to see His Kingdom come on earth as it is in heaven. The ideas and results that we have seen in Brantford did not originate with us. God gave us the ideas, empowered our actions and produced results and undeserved favour beyond what we could imagine. God has given us inspiration, revelation and wisdom every step of the way, combined with undeserved favour in our city. He has shown us secrets on how to bless both the poor and the rich and to love them with no-strings attached.

Along the way, He continually inspires us with stories from the Bible, from history and from our friends around the world who are seeing God do very similar things for them in their context – and He is willing to do the same for you.

God has a plan for your city and He can't wait to share it with you and then partner with you to see it come to pass.

2

THE VISION FOR CITIES

"That's great, God, let's go transform cities!" I said.

"We can't go and do it, Brian, because you love the idea more than you love the people", God replied.

This was a disturbing way for God to attract me to the idea of His heart for city transformation.

It happened one Sunday night in 1995. October 15th, 1995 to be exact. This was the occasion where I would receive what would become the most significant personal experience in our pursuit and passion for city transformation.

At the end of our evening service, I joined many of our church congregation who were already worshipping the Lord at the front of our church. While I was worshipping, some youth came over and began to pray for me. I don't really know who came over, or how long they prayed, but by the end of their prayers God revealed to me the reason why I was there that night.

In what I can only describe as an open vision, the Lord rolled out for me what I would describe as my personal call to cities. The following is what God showed me:

> I was standing at the top of a cliff. In front of me, between myself and the

When was the last time you asked God to show you His heart for your city?

How long has it been since you asked to see the people in your city the way God sees them?

I guarantee you that this will change your perspective and inspire you to partner with God to ask Him to allow you to love them through you.

Brantford was the city that God would call us to in the midst of His dealing strongly with our hearts and motives.

A VISION FOR BRANTFORD

With Sharlyss' emphatic declaration that "we will never go back to that city as long as we live" still ringing in my ears, it seemed fairly certain that Brantford would be the last place to which God would call us. Surely God knew my wife's concerns, right?

As a couple, our custom in making our life decisions has become discussing our options and thoughts about the future, then pray separately about what we were to do in a given situation. Once we were confident that we had heard God we would come back together for further dialogue and prayer together.

The decision to follow God to the city he was calling us to, was no different. I can recall the discussion very clearly:

Brian: "Did you pray and hear from God?"
Sharlyss: "Yes."
Brian: "Do you want to go first?"
Sharlyss: "You won't like my answer."
Brian: "You'll hate my answer!"
Sharlyss: "God said…"
Brian: "Brantford?!"
Sharlyss: "Yes!"
Brian: "Me too!"
Both of us: "Should we pray again?"

Ok, I added that last line for effect. We both knew that God had clearly told us to go to Brantford, a city that up until this moment was not even an option for us.

But God, was very sure that He wanted us in Brantford. Sharlyss, however, needed some assurances before she would make such a move. With a fairly exhaustive list of requests, we moved to Brantford in the fall of 1998 and watched God provide for everything on her list to the smallest detail.

BOMBS AND HORROR MOVIES

We always had an aversion to Brantford but moving to the city proved to be worse than had we imagined. Not long after we moved, my mom came to visit us. One of the first comments she made after driving around the city for a while was, "did a bomb go off in your downtown?" Sadly, the appearance of our downtown did give that impression.

A few years later, film makers from Hollywood came to our city to shoot a movie. The movie was *Silent Hill* – a horror film set in an "eerie and deserted ghost town inhabited by strange beings and a living darkness that literally transforms everything it touches."[2]

It seems that when the news went out from Hollywood California that they were looking for a run-down, eerie, demon-filled city, that the natural answer was for them to travel 2,500 miles and set up in our downtown.

THE WORST DOWNTOWN IN CANADA

Brantford had been a wealthy manufacturing hub in Canada at the turn of the twentieth century. In fact, our city was rated the third largest for economic output in the entire British Empire for manufacturing and industry. The manufacturing base was foundational in the development of a thriving commerce sector in our downtown.

Things changed drastically, however, after the recession of the late 80's and by the early 90's Brantford had become a very depressed and desolate city.

The pervading attitude in the city was 'this is the way we are, and nothing can change.' Young people were growing up, just waiting for their chance to get out of the city. There was little *hope*, few were *prospering*, and the *future* looked bleak.

In 1994, Chris Friel and some of his other young friends felt like they had something to offer the city in terms of new ideas, innovation and energy. So, at 27 years of age he decided to run for office of the Mayor of Brantford. During that first campaign, Chris and his team became known for their courage to face the challenges our city was facing head on. One of the most critical issues at the time was the condition of the downtown.

What had once been known as a thriving and prosperous city core had become neglected and run down.

"We had the Toronto Star, which is a large national newspaper, come into town to look at the downtown to see how bad things had gotten and I said at that time 'this is the worst downtown in Canada,'" Chris said.

The vision articulated by Chris and his team clearly struck a chord with the people of Brantford and they voted him in as mayor of the city. At the time Chris was the youngest mayor in Canada.

REVIVED OR TRANSFORMED?

What our city needed was a revival… or was it?

My favourite course at Bible College was "Revivals". We used to study the great revivals of the past and we wondered together whether it could happen again.

We studied revivals under the leadership of Charles Finney, the Wesley Brothers, George Whitfield and Jonathan Edwards. We researched the first Great Awakening in the 1730's and 40's; the second Great Awakening from 1790 through the 1820's; and the Third Great awakening from 1850 through to the turn of the 20th century. We specifically studied the early 1900's Azusa St. Revival in Los Angeles, California with William Seymour because of its emphasis on the baptism of the Holy Spirit and emergence of the Pentecostal Movement.

The semester of revival studies culminated in a final essay to answer one question from our professor, "Could it happen again?"

While I thoroughly enjoyed the historical research and the knowledge gained of the past, I was left with an uncomfortable assertion that we were relegated to hypothesizing about some potential future visitation. Unfortunately, in the mid 80's in Canada, that was all you could do. Or, so it seemed.

Interestingly, while we were wondering and writing about whether God could do it again, He was already busy doing it in Argentina. This is where our personal story takes another significant shift.

In May of 1999, my wife and I heard that there was going to be a speaker in Toronto who had been very significantly involved in the Argentinian revival. The meetings were held at Toronto Airport Christian Fellowship (now Catch the Fire). The speaker was Ed Silvoso. He was speaking about revival, but more specifically he was talking about how God was transforming cities.

He had written a book on their experiences with revival and transformation called, *That None Should Perish*. The title taken from 2 Peter 3:9 where Peter declares, "The Lord is not slow in keeping his promise, as some understand slowness. Instead he is patient with you, not wanting anyone to perish, but everyone to come to repentance."

They had seen God move in crusades for almost a decade and they had begun to dream with God for Him to transform an entire city. Their stories were based on Biblical principles and strategies and resulted in significant transformation in numerous cities throughout Argentina.

We decided at that conference that we would believe God for our city. If what Silvoso was saying was true, then we agreed that we would commit the rest of our lives to the transformation of cities. This was the beginning of our understanding that transformation is sustainable revival.

Where it seemed that revivals had mainly brought God back into the church where once he had been ignored; transformation would affect both the church and then all of society. The energy needed to keep bringing the church back to life (literally "to re-vive") was much better spent taking all the gospel, to all the city, and seeing all spheres of society transformed.

Although Brantford might have had the "worst downtown in Canada," it was a perfect set-up for God to bring transformation to our unlikely city.

THE VISION

Part of the original vision for Freedom House was that it would eventually have a worship and prayer centre that would be active 24 hours a day, seven days a week. Not long after our launch, one of the original members of Freedom House leadership team, Steve Straza, came across a book that would prove very important in this part of the vision. Some of the key ideas that we would consider incorporating into our church throughout the years, were brought to us by Steve. Steve researches what's happening in both the local and global church like few I know.

The book that he brought to us on this occasion was called Red Moon Rising, by Pete Greig. Red Moon Rising chronicled the origins of their movement, 24/7 Prayer, through England and far beyond.

Pete wrote a poem on a prayer wall many years ago that I believe was a cry from the heart of God for people to see their cities and their call to their cities, the same way that God does.

His poem is called – The Vision[3].

So this guy comes up to me and says, "What's the vision? What's the big idea?"
I open my mouth and words come out like this...
"The vision? The vision is JESUS – obsessively, dangerously, undeniably Jesus.
The vision is an army of young people. You see bones? I see an army.
And they are FREE from materialism. They laugh at 9-5 little prisons. They could eat caviar on Monday and crusts on Tuesday. They wouldn't even notice.
They know the meaning of the Matrix; the way the west was won.
They are mobile like the wind, they belong to the nations. They need no passport... People write their addresses in pencil and wonder at their strange existence.
They are free, yet they are slaves of the hurting and dirty and dying.
What is the vision?
The vision is holiness that hurts the eyes. It makes children laugh and adults angry.
It gave up the game of minimum integrity long ago to reach for the stars. It scorns the good and strains for the best. It is dangerously pure.
Light flickers from every secret motive, every private conversation.
It loves people away from their suicide leaps, their Satan games.
This is an army that will lay down its life for the cause.
A million times a day its soldiers choose to lose that they might one day win the great 'Well done' of faithful sons and daughters.
Such heroes are as radical on Monday morning as Sunday night. They don't need fame from names.
Instead they grin quietly upwards and hear the crowds chanting again and again:
"COME ON!"
And this is the sound of the underground

CITY OF GOD

The whisper of history in the making
Foundations shaking
Revolutionaries dreaming once again
Mystery is scheming in whispers
Conspiracy is breathing...
This is the sound of the underground
And the army is disciplined.
Young people who beat their bodies into submission.
Every soldier would take a bullet for his comrade at arms.
The tattoo on their back boasts "for me to live is Christ and to die is gain".
Sacrifice fuels the fire of victory in their upward eyes. Winners. Martyrs.
Who can stop them?
Can hormones hold them back?
Can failure succeed? Can fear scare them or death kill them?
And the generation prays like a dying man with groans beyond talking, with warrior cries, sulphuric tears and with great barrow loads of laughter!
Waiting. Watching: 24 − 7 − 365.
Whatever it takes they will give
Breaking the rules.
Shaking mediocrity from its cozy little hide.
Laying down their rights and their precious little wrongs.
Laughing at labels, fasting essentials.
The advertisers cannot mold them. Hollywood cannot hold them.
Peer-pressure is powerless to shake their resolve at late night parties before the cockerel cries.
They are incredibly cool, dangerously attractive inside. On the outside? They hardly care.
They wear clothes like costumes to communicate and celebrate but never to hide.
Would they surrender their image or their popularity?
They would lay down their very lives - swap seats with the man on death row - guilty as hell. A throne for an electric chair.
With blood and sweat and many tears, with sleepless nights and fruitless days, they pray as if it all depends on God and live as if it all depends on them.
Their DNA chooses JESUS. (He breathes out, they breathe in.)
Their subconscious sings. They had a blood transfusion with Jesus.
Their words make demons scream in shopping centres.

Don't you hear them coming?
Herald the weirdoes! Summon the losers and the freaks. Here come the frightened and forgotten with fire in their eyes.
They walk tall and trees applaud, skyscrapers bow, mountains are dwarfed by these children of another dimension.
Their prayers summon the hounds of heaven and invoke the ancient dream of Eden.
And this vision will be. It will come to pass; it will come easily; it will come soon.
How do I know? Because this is the longing of creation itself, the groaning of the Spirit, the very dream of God.
My tomorrow is His today.
My distant hope is His 3D.
And my feeble, whispered, faithless prayer invokes a thunderous, resounding, bone-shaking great 'Amen!' from countless angels, from heroes of the faith, from Jesus Christ Himself.
And He is the original dreamer, the ultimate winner.
And that, my friend, is 100% Guaranteed.

❦

HAVE YOU EVER FELT LIKE THE CITY YOU ARE LIVING IN IS AN *UNLIKELY place* for God to bring transformation?

Have you ever considered that maybe *your unlikely place* is the perfect setting for Him to show His grace, power and mercy?

We can testify that God specializes in doing just that. We have found that the worst places are the best places for God to show up because then He gets all the glory.

3

THREE STRIKES AND YOU'RE...?

The Brantford Evangelical Ministerial Association was a network of Pastor's that started in the mid-80's to bring the evangelical Pastors and church together to have a voice in the city. A number of very exciting events and ministries were blessed, and others started because of this group. We were very aware of this network and had partnered with them in the past for some of these events. There was a hunger to see God move in our city.

Having been inspired by Ed Silvoso and the stories of city transformation in his book, "That None Should Perish" we felt like this could help move our association along.

We bought all the materials that weekend - the books, the manuals, the leaders guide, the videos - and brought it back to our Pastors network. The leader of the network agreed that we should start down the path of transformation and so with the information in hand, we set off to transform our city. We started meeting regularly for prayer. Insight from the material, combined with genuine hunger for a move of God grew more and more intense.

CELEBRATION 2000: WONDERFUL NAME, TERRIBLE EVENT

In the fall of that year, the idea of a city-wide evangelistic crusade was brought to the Pastors' Network. We agreed that we would pursue the idea of an event the following year that we would call "Celebration 2000". We began to work diligently, organizing teams, structuring specific evenings, raising money and moving forward. There were lots of meetings and committees and sub-committees, and soon the event had eclipsed the larger vision of city transformation.

By the time *Celebration 2000* came, we had all but forgotten how we had started a year previously and had reduced our vision to a single event. *Celebration 2000* was a wonderful name, but it turned out to be a terrible event.

We had rented the largest venue in the city, which could have held up to 3,000 people, our largest crowd of the week was not much more than 200. With poor attendance and even poorer offerings, Celebration 2000 became a devastating blow to a once exciting transformation movement. The Pastors' Network kept meeting regularly, but trying to bring up the idea of working together for city transformation again, was frowned upon. Strike one.

FRESHWIND 99.5

Not long after this our local Christian Radio Station, Freshwind 99.5 was started. Tony and Vicki Schleifer, a local couple who were involved in both church and marketplace ministry had felt strongly led by God to start this new ministry. I was introduced to them by a mutual friend.

When I sat down with them and shared the vision for city transformation, I was very encouraged to hear that they felt like the radio station could be a great place of unity and declaration for the cause. I agreed to come on staff as one of Freshwind's managers at that time.

In early 2001, Freshwind 99.5 was ready to hire our first morning show host. Up to that point, all of the music and shows on air were pre-recorded and pre-loaded to run automatically. When the Schleifers asked me if I knew anyone in the area who could host the morning show, I recommended Dave Carrol. Dave and his wife Krissy had just returned from 7 months in Ghana, West Africa. I didn't know a lot about Dave except that he had gone to school for broadcasting and that he needed a job.

Dave came on staff at Freshwind 99.5 in January of 2001. It was only a few months later that we would have a conversation that would set up what has now become a significant relationship to the present.

We were discussing another event that we were planning in the city, when Dave was telling me about his exploits in Ghana. When Dave tells this story, he claims that I was ignoring most of what he was saying until the point where he talks about *the book*[1].

Dave was going on about Baseball camps and the heat and African music and... and... and... and then he said, "One day I went looking for something to read at a local Christian book store. The only thing that I saw that looked even remotely interesting was a book by a guy named Ed Silvoso, called *That None Should Perish*."

Dave went on to say that through that book and a series of other interesting coincidences, that the Carrols realized, while in Ghana, that God was calling them back to be ministers and missionaries to Canada. And even more specifically, to work with others to see God transform cities.

Now he had my attention. We talked for hours that day about transformation in Brantford and how God could use the radio station as a non-denominational hub for unity, prayer, and proclamation. We worked together at the station for several years hoping it would be a central and neutral place for transformation.

While we had great favour with the owners and many in the community were desiring to see a greater city-wide movement. Sadly, the leaders of the Brantford Ministerial Association were very reluctant to talk about a unified group to seek for city transformation. Strike two.

JUST WORSHIP

While Dave was hosting the morning show, talking about city transformation as much as he could, I requested the Sunday evening time slot from the owners to do a show that I called *Just Worship*. The pitch to the Schleifer's was that every Sunday night from 9pm until midnight, I would play worship music over the city on the radio airwaves with lots of transformation talk interjected. Then, once a month we would call the worship-

mission to see God's Kingdom come to our cities as it is in heaven. This has to include the integration of business, education, government, and the church working together.
3. **Function:** This is the realization that there is work to do and that it is a shared responsibility.

After many years and several failed attempts to work together, we finally found the missing part of the equation for our city – three steps that we've seen help accelerate the effectiveness of other city-wide transformation networks as well. We agreed that the Lord still had great plans for our city and made the choice to work together in unity to see His will come to pass, but this time we laid the foundation correctly. (We will speak about this more in chapter 8.)

I believe this understanding will be as helpful for you as it was for us and many others, we have shared it with.

Be encouraged! Your desire to transform your community is admirable and truly the heart of God *but* do yourself a favour and learn from our mistakes. Follow the process of unity – first family, then philosophy, and finally function – and watch His favour overwhelm you and your city.

4

THE CITY OF GOD

"What did you see, Marie?" I asked.
"I saw the sign on the highway change from 'Brantford - A River Runs Through It' to 'Brantford - City of God.'"

In the winter of 2000, a few churches had come together for an evening of prayer and worship. One of the ladies from our church, Marie Papple, was given a very specific vision at the end of the evening that became a rallying cry even up to the present day.

I was leading worship that night. Near the end of the service it was clear that the Lord was speaking to Marie about something significant. I walked down off the platform and went straight over to Marie and she told me that the sign now read "City of God."

While it was hard to envision a city with the *"worst downtown in Canada"* as the *"City of God"*, that is what the Lord wanted us to see, declare and work towards.

WHAT IS A "CITY OF GOD"?

For the Jews, the City of God is Jerusalem.
    For some, it's heaven, or the New Jerusalem.
    Others, when they hear the term, think of the work that Augustine

penned as an apologetic masterpiece, *De Civitate Dei* about 413 – 426 AD. Augustine's *City of God* was written in response to pagan claims that the invasion by barbarians in 410 was one of the consequences of the abolition of pagan worship by Christian emperors. St. Augustine responded by asserting to the contrary; "that Christianity saved the city from complete destruction and that Rome's fall was the result of internal moral decay. He further outlined his vision of two societies; that of the elect, *'The City of God'* and that of the damned, *'The City of Man.'* These cities are symbolic embodiments of the two spiritual powers; faith and unbelief, that have contended with each other since the fall of the angels."[1]

For us, *"Brantford, City of God"* was, *and is,* a prophetic declaration of what God wants to do in our city. He wants to make our city, His city. It is a place where God's people are partnering together with each other and with the Lord to bring His Kingdom to "earth as it is in heaven."

We were being invited to partner with the Lord of Glory to bring His Kingdom to *Brantford* as it is in heaven.

When we first started declaring that Brantford was the city of God in 2000, no one else really partnered with us. Almost everyone would say things like:

"Don't you see how bad our downtown is?"

"Can't you see how bad our economy is?"

"Aren't you aware of the major issues that we have in our city?"

The fact was, we did know about all of those issues, but we chose to believe in the Lord's plans over the present conditions. *The truth was* that God was calling us to partner with what *He saw*. His plans and desires for our city far exceeded our own and we chose to come into agreement with God's view of our city. We were "calling those things that aren't, as though they were."[2]

We chose to declare that our city was the city of God.

We still choose this today.

CHANGING THE SPIRITUAL ATMOSPHERE OVER OUR CITY

There are no rewards for being a critic. That's a job anyone can do and too many people settle for it. God is looking for dreamers, strategists and risk takers who can see into the spiritual realm and understand how to bring God's plans from heaven to earth.

We can all agree that the cities in which we live look nothing like the "on earth as it is in heaven" mandate from Jesus. In fact, I believe that the beginning of transformation is directly linked to a Godly discontentment that drives God's people to cry out for Him to move in their city.

POLIPNEUMACLIMATOLOGISTS

Can we agree that there is an expectation on us to respond to the call of the Spirit to believe for more, and to actively participate with God in the transformation of our city?

Polipneumaclimatologists

Poli WHAT?

Polipneumaclimatologists.

Poli = city (Greek origin)

Pneuma = Spirit (Greek origin)

Climatologist = Climatologists are scientists who study the atmosphere of the earth. They collect and analyze data of air, water, soil and plant life to find patterns in the weather. They then use these patterns to predict how the earth and those who live here will be affected by the climate. More simply put, they study the atmosphere to help make those living, have the safest, most productive life possible.

A *polipneumaclimatologist*[3] studies the spiritual atmospheres of their city and makes recommendations of what to do to have the most abundant life possible.

Polipneumaclimatolists ask questions like, "Holy Spirit what are you saying about our city, so we can have the atmosphere of heaven here?"

And, "Holy Spirit how can I partner with you to bring the atmosphere of heaven where it presently does not exist in my city?"

And, "Holy Spirit, what are the right strategies and tactics to participate in the change that you know should happen in my city?"

We found that worship, prayer and the prophetic became significant in the plan to change the spiritual atmosphere over our city.

THERMOMETER OR THERMOSTAT

A thermometer tells the temperature. It's presently 21 degrees in my house. The temperature outside today is 30 degrees.

Thermometers are like the spiritual gift of discernment. You feel or sense something that's in the atmosphere. A spiritual thermometer discerns the spiritual climate. You can tell when something is *not right* or *missing* in a room or certain area of town.

While that is wonderful and important, it is not enough. We have to learn to move from telling the temperature to controlling the temperature. That's what thermostats do.

Thermostats regulate the temperature. You carry the presence of the Spirit (pneuma) and regulate the climate wherever you go.

We live by both checking the temperature and then regulating the temperature.

We can become known as peacemakers in our homes and workplaces and churches by discerning the spiritual climates and then bringing the presence of heaven that regulates the temperature.

Let me add one more step to this process for *polipneumaclimatologists*. In recent years, scientists have learned how to "seed" the clouds with dry ice and silver iodide to make it rain. Read that again, we have learned how to make it rain. Let that speak to you *polipneumaclimatologists*.

We need to be able to discern the spiritual climate, we need to be able to change the climate and we need to be able to make it rain.

God is looking for people who can make it rain!

A RIVER OF TRANSFORMATION

We are privileged to be part of the Transform Our World network, led by Dr. Ed Silvoso. Dr. Silvoso has spent years studying scripture to find both insight and principles on how to bring heaven's culture to earth.

Our journey from first hearing Dr. Silvoso in 1999 to our present-day affiliation to his Transform Our World network has been a remarkable one. We have found ourselves in relationship with the most amazing people from around the globe. This network, led by Ed and Ruth Silvoso fosters authentic relationships, brings biblical and historical validity to city transformation. Ed gives language to the internal heart-cry of the people of God to see a release of His Kingdom in every sphere of society.

The global church owes a tremendous debt of gratitude to the Silvoso's for forging the way with both sound Biblical understanding, and real-life accounts of how God is transforming individuals, industries, cities, and nations around the world.

The remainder of this chapter will be a condensed "Beattie Paraphrase" of Dr. Silvoso's teaching that can be found in expanded form in his books, *Transformation*, *Prayer Evangelism*, and *Ekklesia*.

This would be our understanding of how Jesus wants his church (*Ekklesia*) to bring His Kingdom on earth as it is in heaven. Transformation is like a river that flows in and through cities and nations. Like every river, the river of transformation has two significant banks.

PRAYER EVANGELISM

The one river bank is the lifestyle of Prayer evangelism.

The Biblical foundation for *prayer evangelism* is found in Luke 10.

Luke 10:1-9 After this the Lord appointed seventy-two others and sent them two by two ahead of him to every town and place where he was about to go. [2]He told them, "The harvest is plentiful, but the workers are few. Ask the Lord of the harvest, therefore, to send out workers into his harvest field. [3]Go! I am sending you out like lambs among wolves. [4] Do not take a purse or bag or sandals; and do not greet anyone on the road. [5]"When you enter a house, first say, 'Peace to this house.' [6]If someone who promotes peace is there, your peace will rest on them; if not, it will return to you. [7]Stay there, eating and drinking whatever they give you, for the worker deserves his wages. Do not move around from house to house. [8]"When you enter a town and are welcomed, eat what is offered to you. [9]Heal the sick who are there and tell them, 'The Kingdom of God has come near to you.'

Found specifically in verses 5 through 8; the steps of prayer evangelism are bless, fellowship, meet felt needs, proclaim the Kingdom[4].

To *bless* is *speaking peace* to others. All people are created in God's image which necessitates our willingness to honour and value them regardless of their current spiritual condition. When we bless them, we don't have to agree with what they are doing, but we choose to declare that they are blessed with the Kingdom of God. As *polipneumaclimatologists*, we recognize our authority to bring the atmosphere of heaven to every interaction we have.

For too long the church has been known for what we are *against more than what we are for*. We need to be *for* the people in our cities. We choose to *bless and not blast*.

We fellowship with them. We spend time with others; eating, and drinking, and hanging out with them. You will be surprised how many genuine friendships are developed this way; I was.

We meet their *felt needs*. In the direct context of Luke 10:9 Jesus says, "heal the sick." In the greater context of Luke 10, Jesus tells the story of the Good Samaritan ending with the command to *"go and do the same."* I would suggest that we should expand the understanding of *felt needs* to include *whatever need* is presented. Of course, as Christians we do this in conjunction with what God is specifically saying to us. You will need to discover and minister to the practical needs of the people in your city before you should expect them to open their hearts to you or God.

Finally, in this passage Jesus says, "tell them that the Kingdom of God has come near to you." In the lifestyle of *prayer evangelism*, we call this step *proclaim the Kingdom*. Let's be clear, the most important need of humanity is to recognize our need for a Saviour. When we demonstrate God's love by meeting practical needs we build a platform to declare that the *Kingdom of God has come near to them*. We need to be prepared to share this in a clear and respectful way.

It is important to understand that the order of these steps is significant. Don't jump to the proclamation, without blessing, spending time with others and meeting the real needs in their lives. The lifestyle of prayer evangelism is:

1. Bless
2. Fellowship
3. Meet Felt needs.
4. Proclaim the Kingdom

FIVE PIVOTAL PARADIGMS

The other bank of the river is the understanding of the "five pivotal paradigms"[5] of transformation.

Here they are:

1. *We are called to disciple nations:* The Great Commission is about discipling nations, not just people/individuals. (Matthew 28:19-20)
2. *We are called to reclaim what has been redeemed:* The marketplace which is the heart of the nation, has already been redeemed by Jesus and now needs to be reclaimed by His followers. Jesus has given us everything we need to reclaim both people and systems.
3. *We are all called ministers:* There are no callings more sacred than another. The calling to be part of the *Ekklesia* is level ground for all. Labour is worship
4. *We are called to take the Kingdom everywhere:* We will take the Kingdom of God where the kingdom of darkness is still entrenched in order for Jesus to build His church.
5. *We are called to eliminate systemic poverty:* The premier social indicator that transformation has taken place is the elimination of systemic poverty. *(spiritually, relationally, materially and motivationally)*.[6]

EKKLESIA

Once we understand the importance of both the information and the application of *prayer evangelism and the five pivotal paradigms,* we can then find our role in the *Ekklesia* based on our passions and giftings.

In Matthew 16:18, Jesus said "...I will build my church, and the gates of Hades will not overcome it."

The Greek word for "church" is *Ekklesia* and means "called out" or "selected ones."

Ekklesia is not a religious term, but a political and governmental term that is used many times in classical Greek for a group of people who have been summoned and gathered together to govern the affairs of a city.[7]

The *Ekklesia* were selected and trained up to know the best about the Greek culture, to live and lead this culture by example. The term was understood to mean legislative assembly or city council. These were the best educated and the best leaders of their society. They were the decision makers and the influencers.

For Jesus to use this term means he is giving the keys of governmental authority in his Kingdom to the church. This would have painted a very clear but shocking picture for his disciples; confronting the current religious ideas they had about the continuation of the temple or the synagogue (The two Jewish religious institutions of the day.)

Jesus could have used the word temple which was a place of worship that was understood by his disciples. Jesus could have said he was building a synagogue which was a place of study. But he did not use either of these terms, he used *Ekklesia*.

Jesus was not establishing another building. Instead, he was selecting and training people who would understand the culture and atmosphere of heaven. They would be Jesus' *Ekklesia*[8] who would live and lead with authority in the city. Making it the City of God.

5

CAN YOU NAME THE CITY YOU ARE FIGHTING FOR?

Joshua fought for Jericho, then went after more.
Can you name the city you're fighting for?

THIS IS THE REFRAIN FROM A SONG THAT GOD GAVE ME, DURING A CITY-wide prayer meeting. God was asking us to believe for city transformation. Over and over we sang and declared the words to this song "City of God," believing and contending for it through prayer and worship.

At the time, I was running a city-wide young adult ministry called Genesis. We would often spend extended times of worship and prayer at Genesis and the prophetic declaration *"City of God"* became very significant to us.

City of God also became the banner under which we would worship and pray through the *Just Worship* and *Just Worship Live* events. We chose to partner with what God was saying in the spiritual realm over the city, before we saw anything happening in the natural realm.

THE PROMISED LAND

Do you remember these guys... Shammua, Shaphat, Igal, Palti, Gaddiel, Gaddi, Ammiel, Sethur, Nahbi and Geuel?

Of course, you don't. I have asked this question repeatedly, in many different places where I have spoken, and no one ever knows who they are.

Let me help you, they are Biblical characters that played an important role in the history of Israel.

Still no answer?

Time for Google?

Shammua, Shaphat, Igal, Palti, Gaddiel, Gaddi, Ammiel, Sethur, Nahbi and Geuel are the ten spies that Moses sent out that came back with a report of fear from the Promised Land. They saw the land flowing with milk and honey, but chose to focus on the giants that were going to try to stop them from taking the land.

The other two spies Joshua and Caleb, saw the land and the giants and said, "we are well able to possess what God has promised us."

Joshua, chosen by Moses to lead the people of Israel into the Promised Land, was a man of both vision and courage.

FACE TO FACE WITH GOD

Exodus 33:7-11 Now Moses used to take a tent and pitch it outside the camp some distance away, calling it the "tent of meeting." Anyone inquiring of the Lord would go to the tent of meeting outside the camp. ⁸And whenever Moses went out to the tent, all the people rose and stood at the entrances to their tents, watching Moses until he entered the tent. ⁹As Moses went into the tent, the pillar of cloud would come down and stay at the entrance, while the Lord spoke with Moses. ¹⁰Whenever the people saw the pillar of cloud standing at the entrance to the tent, they all stood and worshiped, each at the entrance to their tent. ¹¹The Lord would speak to Moses face to face, as one speaks to a friend. Then Moses would return to the camp, but his young aide Joshua son of Nun did not leave the tent.

Did you see that?

Moses met God face to face, *but so did Joshua*.

Joshua learned from his great mentor the significance of meeting with

God to hear what His plans were, so he would be able to carry them out with precision.

It's no wonder that Joshua 1 starts with the words "and the Lord said to Joshua."

With this insight, we understand more clearly what happened privately between God and Joshua. Now we can imagine some of the face to face conversations Joshua must have had with God to get specific instruction to win every battle that he would face in the Promised Land.

Now, it makes complete sense that when God tells him how to win every battle that he would face in the Promised Land.

JOSHUA AND JERICHO

All the fighting men have died in the wilderness. Just before they set out for Jericho, God says, "Oh, by the way, you need to circumcise all the men who are going up to Jericho. Then, you can go walk around the city for seven days and on the seventh day, walk around seven times and then shout." (Beattie paraphrase.)

Now, I am not a military strategist, but this seems like a bad plan - except that Joshua had learned to hear God and obey.

Joshua 6:1-20 says, *Now the gates of Jericho were securely barred because of the Israelites. No one went out and no one came in.*

²Then the Lord said to Joshua, "See, I have delivered Jericho into your hands, along with its king and its fighting men. ³March around the city once with all the armed men. Do this for six days. ⁴Have seven priests carry trumpets of rams' horns in front of the ark. On the seventh day, march around the city seven times, with the priests blowing the trumpets. ⁵When you hear them sound a long blast on the trumpets, have the whole army give a loud shout; then the wall of the city will collapse and the army will go up, everyone straight in." ⁶So Joshua son of Nun called the priests and said to them, "Take up the ark of the covenant of the Lord and have seven priests carry trumpets in front of it." ⁷And he ordered the army, "Advance! March around the city, with an armed guard going ahead of the ark of the Lord."

⁸When Joshua had spoken to the people, the seven priests carrying the seven trumpets before the Lord went forward, blowing their trumpets, and the ark of the Lord's covenant followed them. ⁹The armed guard marched ahead of the priests who blew the trumpets, and the rear guard followed the ark. All this time the trum-

pets were sounding. ^{10}But Joshua had commanded the army, "Do not give a war cry, do not raise your voices, do not say a word until the day I tell you to shout. Then shout!" ^{11}So he had the ark of the Lord carried around the city, circling it once. Then the army returned to camp and spent the night there.

^{12}Joshua got up early the next morning and the priests took up the ark of the Lord. ^{13}The seven priests carrying the seven trumpets went forward, marching before the ark of the Lord and blowing the trumpets. The armed men went ahead of them and the rear guard followed the ark of the Lord, while the trumpets kept sounding. ^{14}So on the second day they marched around the city once and returned to the camp. They did this for six days. ^{15}On the seventh day, they got up at daybreak and marched around the city seven times in the same manner, except that on that day they circled the city seven times. ^{16}The seventh time around, when the priests sounded the trumpet blast, Joshua commanded the army, "Shout! For the Lord has given you the city! ^{17}The city and all that is in it are to be devote to the Lord. Only Rahab the prostitute and all who are with her in her house shall be spared, because she hid the spies we sent. ^{18}But keep away from the devoted things, so that you will not bring about your own destruction by taking any of them. Otherwise you will make the camp of Israel liable to destruction and bring trouble on it. ^{19}All the silver and gold and the articles of bronze and iron are sacred to the Lord and must go into his treasury."

^{20}When the trumpets sounded, the army shouted, and at the sound of the trumpet, when the men gave a loud shout, the wall collapsed; so everyone charged straight in, and they took the city.

Amazingly, Jericho was just one of thirty-one cities that God leads Joshua to conquer in his life-time.

Joshua fought for Jericho, then went after more.
Can you name the city you're fighting for?

YOUR CITY, THE CITY OF GOD

Today, I want to encourage you to hear what God is saying over your city. I want to challenge you to see your city the way Jesus does. It's the same strategy that Joshua had for Jericho in Joshua 6. It is a vision of Jesus and what Jesus wants for all cities.

I want to confirm that the burning in your heart right now as you read these words is the Spirit of God drawing you to himself, confirming what you already had hoped and dreamed.

What will it take for you to believe that God wants to make your city, His city?

What are you willing to do to see that His desires are fulfilled in your city? Can you name the city you are fighting for?

6

HEAR GOD AND OBEY

I'm often asked, "What is the most important step in transformation?" and this is it. You have to learn to hear what God is saying and be ready to quickly respond with a *yes!*

Hear God and obey.

It came from a clear rebuke from God that said I wasn't ready to pursue city transformation. But, it was the sweetest rebuke ever. For us, this didn't come without significant intentionality and humility.

It seems that most of us can get into a routine where we think we know what God wants without actually involving Him in the process. It's not uncommon for even good meaning Christians to set our plans and then ask God to bless them, rather than going to God for the plan and the way to unfold the plan.

This is where we found ourselves in the mid-90's. We were midway through our fourth Pastoral position with a lot of other travelling ministry experience as well, when we were faced with an important life decision. We had been trained well to analyze these type of situations, weighing out the pros and cons; get some good counsel from others and, of course pray about it.

What we received from one couple in our lives would change us and how we would do ministry from that point forward.

Barb and Jim Forsdyke were a wonderful, Godly couple. We met them because their son, Jimmy, was attending our youth group. The Forsdykes were on the Prayer Team at Toronto Airport Vineyard Church which had been in the midst of a historic move of God.

One evening the Forsdykes had us over for supper when we began to chat about the decision we were in the middle of processing. We explained our situation, the pros, the cons, our thoughts and feelings when Barb asked us this question, "Have you asked God?"

Our quick response was, "Yes, we're praying about it."

She asked again, "Have you asked God?"

We replied, "Yes. We're praying about it".

A third time she inquired, "Have you asked, God?"

Clearly, we were having a communication problem. Barbara knew exactly what she was saying, and we were very sure that we were both saying the same thing, which could not have been further from the truth.

Praying about something came quite easily to us, but had unknowingly turn into a religious ritual. It was not our intention to exclude God from the process, but neither were we intentional about inviting Him into it.

God's desire for a two-way face to face conversation with us had been replaced with us coming to Him, telling Him what we need and leaving it at that. Let's be honest, a one-way conversation with just us talking is way easier (and less freaky.) The unfortunate truth is; most Christians settle for the one-way route.

The Forsdykes were both biblically insightful and amazingly patient as they started us on a journey of a lifestyle of "hear God and obey."

Over the next number of months, the Forsdykes took great care to teach us the difference between saying prayers to God and having a conversation with God.

They opened up about their journey with God and how He had revealed Himself to them as the One who would lead them very specifically and walk with them very closely. They showed us through the Word and through their lives what a relationship with Holy Spirit could really look like. They assured us that good fathers speak to their children and when invited, our Heavenly Father will prove that He is the best Father ever.

This "hear God and obey" lifestyle became foundational in our personal lives and in all the steps we would take from that point on in our leading in ministry as well.

This is how we ended up in Brantford – hear God and obey.

It's how we made the decision to start Freedom House in Brantford – hear God and obey.

It's why we turned down what looked like better offers elsewhere – hear God and obey.

It's how we ended up buying a bar in the downtown of a depressed city – hear God and obey.

It's the way we lead Freedom House to this very day – hear God and obey.

We believe it is the mandate of every Christian – hear God and obey.

JOSHUA – HEAR GOD AND OBEY

Through the *hear God and obey* lifestyle, we resigned our position in a very large church in Toronto, to move to the city that we used to avoid; Brantford. We pushed through 5 years of obedience in Brantford, without much to show for it externally.

When God said, "it is time", we started our church. Freedom House began with twelve people in our living room. Two months later we were signing a lease-to-own agreement on a bar in a very rough part of our town.

While renovating the bar into our church, we met with our core group to establish the culture of Freedom House. The book of Joshua became our Biblical foundation for discussion during this time. We spent a few months looking at the life and times of Joshua seeing the truth of the phrase over and over again that emphasized the mandate to *hear God and obey*.

Joshua 1:1-9 After the death of Moses the servant of the LORD, the LORD said to Joshua son of Nun, Moses' aide: ²"Moses my servant is dead. Now then, you and all these people, get ready to cross the Jordan River into the land I am about to give to them—to the Israelites. ³I will give you every place where you set your foot, as I promised Moses. ⁴Your territory will extend from the desert to Lebanon, and from the great river, the Euphrates—all the Hittite country—to the Mediterranean Sea in the west. ⁵No one will be able to stand against you all the days of your life. As I was with Moses, so I will be with you; I will never leave you nor forsake you. ⁶Be strong *and courageous, because you will lead these people to inherit the land I swore to their ancestors to give them. ⁷"Be strong and very courageous. Be careful to obey all the law my servant Moses gave you; do not turn from it to the right or to the left, that you may be successful wherever you go. ⁸Keep this Book of the Law always on your lips; meditate on it day and night, so that you may be careful to do everything written in it. Then you will be prosperous and successful. ⁹Have I not commanded you? Be strong and courageous. Do not be afraid; do not be discouraged, for the LORD your God will be with you wherever you go."*

Allow me to summarize:

God spoke.

He gave clear instructions.

He promised success with obedience.

When Joshua listened and obeyed, he was prosperous and successful.

And it's not just in Joshua chapter 1 that God speaks to Joshua:

Joshua 1:1 ... "and the Lord said to Joshua"

Joshua 3:7... "and the Lord said to Joshua"

Joshua 4:1 ... "and the Lord said to Joshua"

Joshua 4:15 ... "and the Lord said to Joshua"

Joshua 5:2 ... "and the Lord said to Joshua"

Joshua 5:9 ... "and the Lord said to Joshua"

Joshua 6:2 ... "and the Lord said to Joshua"

Joshua 6:6 ... "and the Lord said to Joshua"

Joshua 7:10 ... "and the Lord said to Joshua"

Joshua 8:1... "and the Lord said to Joshua"

Joshua 8:18... "and the Lord said to Joshua"

Joshua 10:8... "and the Lord said to Joshua"

Joshua 10:12... "and the Lord said to Joshua"

Joshua 11:6... "and the Lord said to Joshua"

Joshua 13:1... "and the Lord said to Joshua"

And on and on and on.

Every time God spoke, Joshua would turn to the people, and he would repeat what God told them to do and they were quick to obey.

It seems like there might be an important message in all of this.

There are only 2 times recorded in the book of Joshua, where they suffered any type of setback, and both times was because of disobedience.

The first is found in Joshua 7 where Achan disobeys the Lord at Ai.

Joshua is so upset that he's weeping and begging God to have mercy and God tells him to get up and deal with the disobedience in his camp. He does, and God restores the people of Israel.

The other time is found in Joshua 9 where Joshua had made a decision, "without inquiring of the Lord."

Every other time Joshua heard God, obeyed and took the Promised Land as God told him to. The Lord said to Joshua, thirty-one times about thirty-one cities. Joshua was careful to obey, and God made him prosperous and successful. This whole story should be a sign for us. *Hear God and obey*.

This is the pattern throughout the Bible and there isn't a story that doesn't follow this pattern.

When scripture says, "GOD SAID" it means He actually spoke[1]. Joshua recognized the active and living voice of God in his life and responded accordingly.

THE CONDITIONAL IF/THEN PROMISES OF GOD

It's important to realize that although God's love for us is unconditional, his hand of provision and protection are not.

God's word to Joshua was clear. "*If* you are careful to obey, *then* I will make you prosperous and successful."

My job as a child of God is to: *Hear God and obey*.

As a Leadership Team we decided to take this very seriously and literally. We agreed that Christians were meant to walk in a close relationship with God where we heard what He was saying and responded with a "yes". As a team, this meant that all of our decisions about Freedom House were going to be made with us hearing God together.

So, in the beginning of following this process, we would close our eyes, ask very specific questions that could be answered with a "yes" or "no" answer. If you lifted your right hand, you got a *yes*, if you lifted your left hand you got a *no*. We were meticulous with questions and answers and at times, the process seemed mechanical. But, within a few months, the Lord was sharing much more than *yes or no* answers with us. Amazingly, we had unanimous responses almost every time.

To be honest, submitting to this process of making decisions as the

Lead Pastors of Freedom House, often seemed slow and arduous in the early years. But, what it did then, was create a sense of unity and team that was very significant. While we had the Biblical authority to follow God and expect the Leadership Team to follow us, we chose to create a different style of leadership that was based on mutual respect and acknowledgement of God's voice in each of us.

It's been many years since we've processed with God in such a structured, "mechanical" way, but the procedure has remained the same. All of the decisions that we make at Freedom House are made by listening to Holy Spirit and following His path. Looking back now and seeing our Leadership Team lead their teams and also their families in this lifestyle is one of the greatest gifts that the Lord has given to us.

EARS TO HEAR

It was also during this time that Sharlyss started to meet regularly with a number of our key ladies to teach them to hear God in a more intimate setting. Sharlyss called this group "Ears to Hear" and to this day we still hear stories of how significant this was in those ladies' lives.

It cannot be overstated, how significant both the "Ears to Hear" group; plus the lifestyle of "ears to hear" (*hear God and obey*) has been to Freedom House. Sharlyss' leadership in this lifestyle, combined with her tenacity to see all of Freedom House participate, are foundational to seeing freedom come to individuals and then to various spheres of influence in our city. Transformed people, transform cities.

I am convinced that when we get to heaven, we will see how every good thing that happened in and through us to Brantford, came because of Sharlyss' deep love for God (to have *ears to hear* what He was saying) and her persistent encouragement for us to respond lovingly and obediently to what He had said.

"WHEN GOD CLOSES A DOOR, SOMEWHERE HE OPENS A WINDOW"

In the movie, *Sound of Music*, there is a scene where Maria (Julie Andrews) is in Mother Superior's office. Maria had just returned to the convent after having been governess to the Von Trapp family children. Maria had fallen in love with Captain Von Trapp and had run back to the convent to hide her feelings. Mother Superior insisted that Maria return; she had to face her feelings before she could make any permanent decision to take her vows to be a nun. In the next scene, Mother Superior quotes the famous words: "When God closes a door, somewhere He opens a window." Then, Mother Superior sings, "Climb Every Mountain", much of which is sang in front of an open window, to push the spiritual analogy further for the viewer.

A beautiful movie, with beautiful imagery, and a lovely touching story, but it's terrible theology. Yet, it has become the gospel truth for some in the church today.

When does God ever promise to open a window if He shuts a door?
Maybe God wanted the door shut, so we couldn't go through it.
Maybe He shut it to see how much resilience you have to keep going.
Perhaps it was shut for you to find out why door handles were made?
A closed door could mean many things, but how would you ever know if you can't ask God for a specific answer?

HOW ABOUT A FLEECE?

If it's not doors and windows, sometimes well-intentioned Christians talk about and suggest we should use a *fleece* with God. At least this is more biblical, but still a poor choice for Spirit-filled Christians.

The idea of a fleece is found in Judges 6 where Gideon asks God for confirmation after He has already spoken a direct Word to him.

Judges 6:36 - 40 *"If you will save Israel by my hand as you have promised— [37] look, I will place a wool fleece on the threshing floor. If there is dew only on the fleece and all the ground is dry, then I will know that you will save Israel by my hand, as you said." [38] And that is what happened. Gideon rose early the next day; he squeezed the fleece and wrung out the dew—a bowlful of water. [39] Then Gideon said to God, "Do not be angry with me. Let me make just one more request. Allow me one more test with the fleece, but this time make the fleece dry and let the ground be covered with dew." [40] That night God did so. Only the fleece was dry; all the ground was covered with dew.*

God calls Gideon a mighty man of valour and tells him that he is going to give his people a mighty victory, but in his fear and insecurity Gideon asks for a sign.

"If you're going to save my people and use me to do it, would you mind proving it by having the dew get my fleece wet but keep the ground dry under it tonight?" (Beattie paraphrase)

So, God did it.

"Ok, just one more time, to be really sure. Maybe tonight you could keep my fleece dry, while the ground around it is wet?" (Beattie paraphrase)

And God did it.

While the end of the story sees Gideon winning the battle, it would have been so much better if Gideon had believed who God said he was, heard the plan of the Lord and followed through with it.

With this said, *fleeces* still get brought up way too much today when Christians are discussing what God is saying to them, and how they should respond.

IS IT GOD? IS IT ME? OR IS IT THE DEVIL?

I still remember one of the most freeing statements that I have ever heard in respect to being led by the Spirit and hearing God and obeying. It was a sentence that John Arnott made at a Catch the Fire Conference over twenty years ago. He was speaking about the desire that all Christians have to hear from God and want to obey.

What if it's my own thoughts and not God's?

What if I'm wrong?

What if it's the devil speaking?

John carefully and biblically broke down all the excuses and reasons that Christians give for not following the voice of the Lord, and then he said this, "we must have more faith in God's ability to lead us, then the devil's ability to deceive us." And with that one line, I decided that I was going to press into hearing God and obeying as a lifestyle.

Romans 8:14 says that those *led by the Spirit are the Sons of God.*

Galatians 5:25 instructs us to live by *keeping in step with the Spirit.*

The Book of Acts is really the acts of the Holy Spirit through the apostles. It is safe to say from these scriptures that God spoke and is still speaking by his Spirit. We have the Holy Spirit in us to lead us into freedom.

Hearing God and *obeying* is *normal behaviour* for a Christian.

THE TRUTH WILL SET YOU FREE

Jesus said, "You will know the truth and the truth will set you free". It's a wonderfully encouraging verse for Christians that love to quote it as unconditional promise from our Lord. While it is a wonderful promise, it is not unconditional. Jesus, himself puts His conditions on this.

The promise is found in *John 8:32* "*...you will know the truth, and the truth will set you free."*

However, the verse actually starts with, *"then".*

"Then you will know the truth, and the truth will set you free."

If there's a "then" in scripture, there's a good chance there's an "if" as well.

Look at the verse just before it: *John 8:31 Jesus said, "if you hold to my teaching, you are really my disciples."*

There's the "if". "*If* you hold to my teaching".

There's a Seinfeld episode where Jerry and Elaine are at the car rental agency. Jerry had pre-booked a car and they have come to get the car. Jerry walks up to the desk and gives his name and type of car he had reserved to the lady working at the rental car company.

Then the following conversation occurs[2]:

Lady: Let's see here. I'm sorry we have no mid-sized cars available at the moment.

Jerry: I don't understand; I made a reservation. Do you have my reservation?

Lady: Yes, we do. Unfortunately, we ran out of cars.

Jerry: But, the reservation keeps the car here. That's why you have the reservations.

Lady: I know why we have reservations.

Jerry: I don't think you do. If you did, I'd have a car. See, you know how to *take* the reservations, you just don't know how to *hold* the reservation. And that's really the most important part of the reservation – *the holding*. Anybody can just take them.

"You can take the reservation; you just can't hold the reservation."

"Taking the reservation" for Seinfeld is the equivalent to "hearing the teaching" for us. There's no real benefit in taking the reservation, if you can't hold the reservation. In the same way, there is no real significance in hearing what Jesus is saying, if we are not willing to obey what he says.

The important piece is the holding to the teaching, which is obedience.

Hear God and obey.

THE "SHEMA"

Once we understand the Jewish meaning of the word *hear* it should clarify and confirm everything we've been looking at and give a new outlook on our relationship with God.

"Hear, O Israel: The Lord our God, the Lord is one. You shall love the Lord your God with all your heart and with all your soul and with all your might." (Deuteronomy 6:4,5.)

These words are the beginning of a daily Hebrew prayer that has been part of Jewish belief for thousands of years. It is called "The Shema" and begins with the words *"Hear, O Israel."*

To *hear* for a Jewish reader, came with the understanding and expectation that they were going to respond to what they were hearing. Hearing, in fact, was actually equated with obeying.

Literally what it meant was that when I heard the word of the Lord, that obedience was implied.

Hear God and obey.

OBEDIENCE IS SUCCESS

While we have established the *hear God and obey* portion of Joshua's story, I want to leave you with one more concept from his life that is as significant to us today as it was to him.

We started with, "and God said to Joshua", which is the *hear God* part.

We saw through Joshua's life that every time he was obedient to what God said that he was victorious, which is the *obey* part.

The promise to Joshua was, "if you are careful to obey what I've said, then I will make you successful." In fact, God repeats that twice as recorded in Joshua 1:7 & 8.

Joshua 1:7-8 "Be strong and very courageous. Be careful to obey all the law my servant Moses gave you; do not turn from it to the right or to the left, that you may be successful wherever you go. ⁸Keep this Book of the Law always on your lips; meditate on it day and night, so that you may be careful to do everything written in it. Then you will be prosperous and successful.

I want to suggest from this that the success for the Christian today, like it was for Joshua is actually walking in obedience.

Read this out loud – OBEDIENCE IS SUCCESS.

Read it again – OBEDIENCE IS SUCCESS.

Obedience is success.

Did I hear God?

Did I obey?

If I answered "yes" to both of those questions, then I have been successful.

Success is not a big church, or a big business, or a big house – although God isn't against any of those things.

Failure is not a small church or a small business – failure is failing to ask God and then do what He says.

The most terrific thing about this truth is that we can confidently do our part by hearing and obeying and then we leave the results to God. Sometimes we see the final picture and sometimes we don't, but we can always trust the One with whom we are building. He will take our faithful acts of obedience, breathe on them and turn them into a transformational masterpiece.

HEAR GOD AND OBEY

It is the central theme of scripture for those who want to walk in the continual blessings of God, which makes it a major theme for those who want to see their city transformed.

God wants to see His Kingdom come to your city. He has good plans for this to happen, and He is looking for disciples that will come into agreement with Him by hearing His plans and obeying.

Let me tell you in case you are wondering; you don't know enough by yourself to transform your city. You're not smart enough. You don't have enough insight or foresight. You can't think through the pros and cons and come up with the right answers. Windows, doors and fleeces won't do the trick.

If you could have done it yourself, you would have done it already.

Real Kingdom transformers must learn to hear what the Father is saying and be quick to obey. It's the biblical mandate, and it's the present-day reality.

7

FREEDOM HOUSE - A MINISTRY CENTRE WHERE CHURCH HAPPENS

Coming into 2003, the word from the Lord to us was "it is time." We believed that meant it was time to start Freedom House. For a decade we had been dreaming and making plans as to what it would look like. So, when God said "it is time" we were ecstatic.

January, February and March went by and we kept hearing "it is time" from God and through various other confirmations, but nothing was materializing in the natural. At the beginning of April, I said to Sharlyss, "I'm going to fast and pray for a month and at the end of April we're either going to start our church or find another city to start it in." At the end of the month, we knew that leaving wasn't an option if we were to remain obedient to what God had said. Without a clear next step, we chose to obey God, stay in Brantford and wait for further instructions.

It was the last weekend of May that things picked up significantly. Sharlyss had gone shopping and on the way out of the store felt inclined to pick up a Real Estate magazine that was at the exit of the store. She came home where I was sitting on the couch reading when she proceeded to throw the Real estate magazine at me.

"What's that for?" I asked.

"God told me to give it to you," she said, laughing.

"Did He tell you to deliver that way?" I asked. And we laughed and laughed, (ok, maybe I was the only one who laughed.)

In spite of my flippant reaction, I immediately started scanning to see if indeed God had sent this magazine to me air mail. Within a few minutes, one of the ads *jumped off the page*. Without thinking too much about it, I put the magazine down, grabbed the keys to our Jeep and went off to find that building.

It wasn't long before I was parked in front of one of the ugliest buildings I think I had ever seen. It was a bar called "The Scene" that was only a few minutes from our house. I parked the Jeep, walked up the steps past the two bouncers who were standing there and stood for a moment in the front foyer of the bar. I took a quick right turn and found myself standing at one end of the dance floor. The music was blaring, the bass was pumping, the lights were flashing, the people were drinking and dancing. While taking in all the sights and sounds, immediately I felt the tangible presence of God. It surprised me a bit, because it was unexpected. So, I stood there for a few minutes, still watching, still listening, and still experiencing the presence of the Holy Spirit in that space. When I felt released, I walked around the rest of the bar, checking out several other rooms, eventually finding the main bar area where the owner was serving. I had a quick chat with him, thanked him for his time and left. I was home 3 minutes later.

"So, what did you find?" Sharlyss asked.

"I found one of the buildings in this magazine you threw at me a few minutes ago. It's very interesting. You should go and check it out."

I gave her the address and told her nothing else about what I had experienced.

Sharlyss took the keys to the Jeep and drove to the bar. She walked past the bouncers into the foyer of the bar, then turned right and stood looking at the dance floor where she too *FELT THE TANGIBLE PRESENCE OF GOD.*

She was home within a few minutes, telling me about her experience, which was identical to mine. Now, we aren't the most brilliant people in the world, but we do know when God might be up to something. Later that night we took Dave and Krissy Carrol through the bar and shared with them what had happened to us earlier that evening.

The following week, I set up an appointment with the owner of the bar and asked him if I could rent it for a Sunday night in the middle of June. He agreed. We gathered about 25 people around a pool table in the back room of *The Scene* and shared our vision of what Freedom House would look like. 12 of that group began meeting in our home immediately to form our first leadership team.

On August 1, 2003, we signed a one-year lease-to-own agreement for us to buy that bar. We had a hand full of people, no money, a big dream and a word from the Lord. September first we got the keys to the bar and immediately began renovations in preparation to officially open in December.

The first weekend of September 2003 was one of the most interesting and memorable weekends of my life. On Saturday night the building was a bar, then on Sunday night we had our first gathering as a core team. Monday night we were in the building starting our renovations when there was a knock on the front door. I went to the door, opened it and I got propositioned on the front door of my church. One of the local *ladies of the evening* was apparently hoping for some business. After she left, I turned around to one of our guys who had seen the whole thing and said, "I didn't take this course at Bible College!" A phrase that would become very common over the next few months.

Renovating an old bar is not as glamourous as it sounds, and this bar was far more challenging than you can imagine.

None of the fixtures in the kitchen worked. The stove was unusable, so the previous owners had a BBQ in there instead. The floors everywhere were a sticky mess. The ceiling in the main room was covered in about an inch of dirt. The men's bathroom had so many holes in the walls that the previous owner had stopped trying to patch them with dry wall, but instead had put sheet metal on the walls. The sights and smells of years of drinking, fighting and neglect were everywhere (not to mention, the spiritual cleansing that was needed as well).

THE BASEMENT ANGEL

Night after night, and every Saturday we had teams of people at our new bar, cleaning, fixing, and painting. There was one night that we would never forget. Just outside the door of the kitchen there was a hatch in the floor that opened up to allow access to the basement. It was not a large hatch, probably 4 x 4 feet square, and it opened to reveal a flight of very steep wooden steps that took you to a damp, dirt floor 10 feet below.

We had been working late into the evening and for whatever reason, someone left the hatch door open. Unaware, one of our ladies came through the swinging door of the kitchen, took 2 steps and fell down the hole to the basement. Several of us heard the commotion and by the sounds we were very sure what had happened. It was one of our greatest concerns that this type of thing could occur. We rushed over to the hatch expecting the worst, but surprisingly found the lady just sitting there on the edge of the basement access.

"What happened, Gwen?" we asked.

"Well, I came through the kitchen door and fell down the basement hole. But, I only fell about 3 or 4 feet into the hole when something caught me and threw me back up. I think it was an angel."

Two other Freedom House ladies were right there to witness the odd reversal of gravity and testify to God's hand of protection.

Nicki Straza, one of our ladies who saw the whole thing, recalls the incident as follows:

"I heard Gwen yell and saw her feet fly out from under her as she began to fall. She was disappearing into the hole, but suddenly she reappeared and landed on the far side. Immediately I thought, 'gravity doesn't work that way, maybe one of our guys was in the basement and pushed her up to safety'. But, when we looked there was no one in the basement. It must have been an angel."

The truth is, there is no other reasonable explanation for what happened that night. We had prayed through the building and invited angels to come and partner with us. Apparently, one of them was a Basement Angel.

JUST WORSHIP

Freedom House was officially started in December of 2003. From the beginning, we believed God wanted to create a prototype of transformation. With that in mind, we had no idea how to reach that goal, nor any guarantee it would ever happen.

God had brought together a great team to start Freedom House. We had vision and passion and were ready to start into the transformation of our city immediately. But, God had another plan for the beginning stages of our story. Rather than work and outreach to the city, God clearly asked us to *just worship*.

We worshipped for a month, then 6 months, then a year, then 2 years. For 2 years at the beginning of our new church plant, almost the entire time was spent together worshipping. It was during this time that we pressed deeply into hearing the voice of God and preparing ourselves to respond quickly to what He was saying.

Worship, prayer and the presence of Jesus are still our primary callings at Freedom House. Everything else we do flows out of time with the Father, in His presence, hearing His heart and doing only those things He calls us to do.

FUSION

After the two-year window of *just worship*, we stepped out into other ministries, both inside and outside the church. When this happened, we wanted to be intentional about setting a night aside for only worship. Fusion is the name we gave to that night. That's the sole agenda for the evening.

In the midst of this, we often take time in a worship context to help others recognize how God speaks. We acknowledge God's desire to encourage the body of Christ and how He will use anyone who will step out of their comfort zone to hear and then speak life to others.

FLIPPIN' FRIDAYS

One Sunday night after our service a few of us stayed behind to talk through some church issues. The discussion went late into the evening, so at about 11:30 pm we came out the front door of the church where we were finishing up our discussion and getting ready to leave. While we were standing there, about six or eight kids who looked to be about ten or twelve years old assembled across the street from us, just sitting there on their bikes. We made a couple of comments to ourselves about needing protection from this "local bike gang", but the reality of why they were there was maybe worse than that.

Across the street from our church there was a crack house. It had been known for years (over 30 years we would find out later) that this location was a place that ran drugs locally. As we stood outside our church that evening, we watched people come out of the front door of the crack house, give a quick whistle, which prompted one of the young boys to ride over, grab a bag out of the man's hands and ride off into the Brantford night. We stood and watched this scene repeat itself numerous times that evening as eventually all the boys went off into the evening, used as mules for the drug dealers.

We were stunned, and angry, and concerned, but we didn't know what to do.

I prayed and asked God to send us an evangelist.

He said, "Do the work of an evangelist."

We still didn't know what to do, but we did know that kids running drugs for local crack houses was not acceptable in *our neighbourhood*. We had no real experience in closing down crack houses (that was not a course at Bible College either), but we knew we had to do something. We decided that our strategy to get in the middle of this issue was to start a neighbourhood barbeque, we called it Flippin' Fridays. Every Friday night we would set a free, no-strings-attached BBQ in front of our church from 10pm until 2 or 3 in the morning.

We called the evening Flippin' Friday which we thought was a creative name. Not long after we started, we heard that the people in the neighbourhood called it the "pimp, prostitute and politician BBQ" because that was who was showing up.

Pimps and prostitutes showed up before their shifts that evening. Politicians would come by for a photo opportunity to be seen as one who wants to be part of the homeless, needy solution of our city. Eventually anyone and everyone felt comfortable coming together for a late-night burger, conversation and hope.

It took a while, but eventually we were able to impact the lives of those around us. Several of the men who had been caught in the drug lifestyle became friends and we helped them make better choices for them and their families. Ladies who were caught in the sex industry were given hope and dignity and were helped to make positive course corrections for their lives.

We will tell more of our Flippin' Friday stories in Chapter 8.

LEADING WITH KINDNESS

We had chosen from the very beginning, that we would be a strong community-minded church. We had been inspired deeply by the *Dream Center* in Los Angles, California and by the *Transform Our World* network under the leadership of Dr. Ed Silvoso.

Dr. Silvoso's teaching from Luke 10 in his book *Prayer Evangelism* laid out a clear Biblical methodology from Jesus of how to reach cities. The understanding of finding felt needs and meeting them was our agreed upon method of outreach.

The simple methodology here is:

- Bless
- Fellowship
- Minister
- Proclaim[1].

At Freedom House, we call this the B.E.S.T. life which stands for:

- Bless
- Eat
- Show
- Tell

Our primary method by which we *show* God, would be through practical acts of kindness. After all, Romans 2:4 tell us that it is the kindness of the Lord that leads us to him.

CANADA DAY

One day I got a call from Lori-Dawn Cavin. Lori-Dawn was a lady from our city's Parks and Recreation department. She had heard that we had a

Saturday morning kids' program and she had a need at one of the larger city events for someone to come and help her. That event was Canada Day, the largest event that happens in our city every year.

"Would Freedom House be willing to come and help run the kids' stage at Canada Day this year?" was her request.

And we said "Of course we can!"

Here's a recommendation for those who wish to make an impact in their city to bring tangible transformation. Build relationship with people who are already doing something, ask how you can bless them and be ready to say "yes".

We served the city at Canada Day for a couple of years and then Lori-Dawn made another request.

MOVIES IN THE SQUARE

"Brian, you know that the city has built Harmony Square in our downtown, right?"

I said. "Yes."

"Well," she continued, "I have been given the task of getting people to come downtown and use Harmony Square. Do you think Freedom House would be able to help us put on family movie nights in the Square this summer?"

And I said, "Yes."

That summer we hosted and helped run movies every Thursday night for the summer months. The following year we got the same request.

"Would Freedom House come and help us run Movie Nights in the Square again this summer?"

And I said, "Yes."

Half way through the second summer of movie nights, Lori-Dawn asked me to come to the Parks and Recreation Department offices to meet with her. She had another request.

FROSTY FEST

"Brian, we want to thank you and Freedom House for how you've served with us and how you're helping to create a new culture in our downtown.

We were wondering about doing another event in Harmony Square this winter. Do you think you could do a winter carnival?"

And I said, "Of course we can."

Then I went back to the Freedom House Leadership Team.

"I met with Lori-Dawn again this week, she asked if Freedom House could do a winter carnival and I said, 'yes'. Does anyone have any experience doing a winter carnival?"

I already knew that the answer to that question was, "No."

So, we googled "Winter Carnivals" and found out where the big carnivals in Canada were taking place. We learned as much as we could from their web-sites, then made relationships with a group from Sarnia, Ontario (about 2 hours from us) that had been running a winter carnival for over 20 years. This group was very helpful and to this day we still hire 2 or 3 of them to come and do ice-carving at our winter carnival – Frosty Fest.

Our goal for Frosty Fest for the first year was 1000 people to attend our event. Since our downtown had been ignored and run down for so long and was really still in the rebuilding stages, we thought 1000 would be a wonderful turn out. Well, 8000 people showed up that year.

Year 2: 10,000 people came.

Year 3 & 4: 12,000 people came.

Year 5: 15,000 people came. That year Mayor Chris Friel declared that Frosty Fest was the "watershed moment of the transformation of our downtown."

But he didn't stop there. Mayor Friel went on and said the following.

"Do you know why Freedom House hosts this event every year for the city?"

No one answered.

He continued, "Because they want to show you the love of God in a practical way."

What an amazing statement. I couldn't have said it any better. In fact, I would have given that exact answer, because that is our answer all the time when people stop and ask us why we do so many things in our city. We always say, "Because we want to show you the love of God in practical ways."

We do this because this is what people understand. They may not understand our theology, or our doctrine or our ways of worship, but everyone can understand *the love of God done in practical ways.*

It is the perfect outflow of Matthew 5:18 that says *"let your light shine before others, that they may see your good deeds and glorify your Father in heaven."*

When we can connect kindness to a practical expression of God's love (good deeds) we are rebuilding a lost image of a good God in people's minds.

We're still running Frosty Fest. It has become one of the largest yearly events in our city and one of the largest winter carnivals in all of Canada.

When the city calls, whenever possible, answer with a "YES".

THE LIVING NATIVITY

Since we had now served and honoured the city for several years, Lori-Dawn Cavin came back to me a few months later.

And she said, "Brian, do you have any ideas of other things we could do in Harmony Square?"

We talked for a while and eventually I said, "Lori-Dawn, how about an event around Christmas time? Why don't we do, *The Living Nativity* in Harmony Square in December?"

She said, "What's a Living Nativity?"

Trying to be as un-religious as possible, I replied, "Well, *The Living Nativity* is the Biblical Christmas story of the first Christmas when Mary and Joseph came to Bethlehem, where baby Jesus was born. Then the Shepherds come and say, 'we really like your baby', and the Wisemen come and they say, 'we really like your baby' and the angels sing really nice songs about baby Jesus. What about that?"

Lori-Dawn said, "Give me a week, I'll need to talk to my boss about this one."

Two days later Lori-Dawn called me back. "Brian, we're going to do *The Living Nativity* in Harmony Square this year."

Amazingly, our city was in the middle of a bit of an *atheist/Christian* battle about whether Christian displays should be allowed on city property. More specifically, there was a big fight in our city about whether the large plastic Nativity set should be allowed to stay in Victoria Park, just around the corner from Harmony Square. So, while the battle raged about plastic

Mary, Joseph and Jesus in Victoria Park, we were busy making plans to bring the Living Nativity to Harmony Square – and we did.

After the success of the Living Nativity the first year, Lori-Dawn and I would end our email correspondence with IRLYB for "I REALLY LIKE YOUR BABY". I actually wrote that line right into the play.

One of our favourite stories from the Living Nativity comes from the very first year we did the play. Lori-Dawn and her husband had brought their twin girls (age 7) to our first performance. The girls loved it so much that they insisted that they return for each performance (we do 6 performances each year) and arrived early so they could sit in the front row. They were enthralled by what was happening on stage and seemed to be soaking up every bit of the story.

What happened at the Cavin family Christmas two weeks later is what makes this story so great. After dinner the 2 girls and their cousins went downstairs. A couple of hours had passed and it seemed like it had been a bit too quiet in the basement. Lori-Dawn and her husband, Scott were beginning to wonder what was happening. They went to check on the kids, but were told by the twins that they needed to wait for a few more minutes. An hour later, the girls called them down and proceeded to act out the entire Living Nativity, doing all the parts, singing all the songs and telling the real reason for the Christmas season. They even went so far as to dress up one of the cousins as the donkey that brought Mary into Bethlehem to mimic the live donkey we use in our own performances.

It was this experience that brought the entire Cavin family back into connection with God and back to church.

A MINISTRY-CENTRE WHERE CHURCH HAPPENS

Freedom House is a *ministry centre where church happens*. We coined this phrase, so we could quickly describe Freedom House for those who asked. While we understand that *the church* is *the Ekklesia* – which is always people and never buildings – we have come to realize that this is a deeper teaching than most people have. For most, the *churchy part* is what happens inside the building (services, teaching, etc.). We intentionally lead with what we are called to do in the city – the *ministry part,* where we meet the practical needs of people to show them the practical love of God.

We keep this vision always before us because we want to remember that we are called to love God, love each other, love the city and love extravagantly.

It's unlikely that you are going to go into the downtown of your city and buy a dirty, old, bar and start a ministry-centre there or organize a winter carnival or invent a local superhero.

What you can and should do is contextualize what being intentional about what transformation looks like for your city. The principles that are the same. God's word is the same.

What it looks like and how it rolls out in your city, region or nation could be very different.

So, live a Luke 10 lifestyle of *prayer evangelism (bless, eat, show and tell)*, understand the Biblical foundation of transformation (5 Paradigms), and learn to *hear God and obey*. Then, in the context of the needs of your city, ask God which specific issues He is calling you to resolve.

Say "Yes."

Then, serve God and your city with all your might.

8

THE KINDEST CITY IN CANADA

"*Mr. Speaker, eight years ago, Freedom House, a church and Ministry Centre in Brantford began on a mission called the Kindness Project to see if a city could be transformed 'by good into good' using simple, but strategic acts of kindness. In these eight years, among others things, roughly 20,000 hamburgers have been given away; a free Winter Carnival: Frosty Fest is hosted; a school curriculum is in the works; Affordable Housing has been built providing for those in need; a local Superhero, Captain Kindness has emerged (here, here) and taken control of the city; and this Friday, November the 4th will be the 2nd annual Random Act of Kindness Day in Brantford. The Kindness Project seeks to uncover the untapped level of synergy in our community as a collective commitment to serving each other, it is people helping people with what we all have in our hands to give. Mr. Speaker, we hope, together, to make Brantford known as the KINDEST CITY IN CANADA*".

These were the words of our local Member of Parliament, Phil McColeman in Ottawa, our nation's capital, speaking about what had been accomplished in our city to that point. We were so excited when he called and said he wanted to highlight Freedom House in Parliament.

KINDNESS PROJECT

The Kindness Project is the name we gave to the ongoing, growing list of community outreaches that we were doing in Brantford. The ultimate vision is having a proactive network of individuals and groups in our city that are meeting the practical needs of those in our community in a caring and kind way. We really do intend on having the "kindest city in Canada."

We knew before we started Freedom House that the primary outreach model we would use, would be what had become known as Random Acts of Kindness (RAKs). A few years earlier, I had read a book by Steve Sjogren called, *The Conspiracy of Kindness* which told the story of how God had used his church in Cincinnati through various outreach ideas based in kindness. We had engaged in similar methods at a previous church and found them to be very effective.

Truth be told, the phrase "Random Acts of Kindness" is somewhat misleading in this context. We have found that kindness needs to be both intentional and continual as both a lifestyle and ministry model. We have come to realize that *whoever shows up and stays the longest, wins.*

Our culture does not believe that God is good or kind. Seeing no-strings-attached kindness in God's people undermines an incorrect understanding of who God is and opens doors of hope for them to discover God's love for them.

Kindness has indeed become part of the winning equation.

CAPTAIN KINDNESS IS BORN

It was a hot and muggy August day and we were doing a $1 Car Wash in front of our church. When we say "$1 Car Wash" we are speaking of an outreach event where we give our guests a dollar for the honour of serving them (then, we watch their brains explode.)

I was watching our team members trying to convince drivers to pull into our parking lot for us to wash their cars. They were very enthusiastic, jumping up and down and waving our CAR WASH posters as people drove by. I was getting a bit impatient as too many of the cars were just driving by. I walked over to our Children's Pastor and said to her, "Nicki, we need a mascot; a character in bright colours that people can't ignore."

The following month, our city announced the theme for the Santa Clause Parade for that year. The theme was *Superheroes*. At our staff meeting the following week, we met together and decided we were going to invent a Superhero named Captain Kindness.

We made plans to enter a Captain Kindness float into the parade that year. We partnered with a local trucking company and got an eighteen-wheeler with a 52-foot flatbed trailer to use. On the flatbed, we built a miniature Gotham City with high rises and big city buildings. Standing on the tallest building overlooking the city, was our superhero, Captain Kindness. He was declaring that we could transform our city "By good, into good with Kindness."

It turned out to be an amazing float. In fact, we won the award for best theme float of that year's parade. But, the greatest win was something that we had no way of anticipating. Within weeks we were getting calls from social agencies, schools, and other churches asking if they could have Captain Kindness come and speak at their functions.

God had confirmed that kindness would be an answer to a cultural felt need in our city.

Now, Captain Kindness is recognized everywhere. He hosts many of the public events including: Canada Day, Movies in the Square, New Year's Eve in the Square and others. He has emerged, not just as our Freedom House mascot, but as a personification of what many (In both the church and the marketplace) are endeavouring to see become reality in our community.

Lori-Dawn describes it this way, "Wherever he arrives, you can feel the whole atmosphere of an event change immediately. It's amazing really."

I often say that I'm the only Pastor in the world who has a superhero on staff.

WWCKD?

As part of the Kindness Project we MC the city's free *Movies in the Square* program. This is a free family night in Harmony Square every Thursday evening throughout the summer months. Prior to the movie, Captain Kindness and his Kindness Crew run a program for the kids that includes games, skits, and RAKs.

One evening, Captain Kindness was finished his movie night pre-show and he was heading back to our church from the Square which is about a two-minute walk through an alley way past a local bar. The Captain calls this walk the "gauntlet" because invariably there will be a number of people sitting on the patio of the bar having a few pints seemingly waiting for him to come by, so they can taunt him a little. As he was walking by, prepared for his usual barrage of comments, one particular man asked if he could speak to him for a minute.

He said, "Captain I have to tell you this story. I was heading to work this morning and I saw a homeless guy on the street asking everyone for money for food. He asked me too as I passed him. I wasn't going to stop or do anything for him, but then I thought 'What would Captain Kindness do?' and I knew I had to do something. So, I stopped, and I took him out for breakfast. I just wanted you to know that, Captain." With that, he sat back down and took another sip of his beer.

"By good into good" as the Captain would say.

FLIPPIN' FRIDAYS

As previously mentioned, the area of town where we started Freedom House was quite a challenge. Flippin' Fridays became our way of building relationships and meeting some of the practical needs there. Here are some stories from Flippin' Fridays through the years.

"Do you Want a Burger?" (written by Dave Carrol)

On this particular Friday night, the summer heat turned into thunderstorms and we moved the social part of Flippin' Fridays inside our church. As the inside bustled about, I sat on a bar stool getting wet in the alley minding the grill. As usual I was hollering "Free Burgers!" at passersby, waiting to see who God wanted to draw into His "Holy Ghost Tractor Beam."

Soon after, a pair of young men walked past very intently in the dark. I yelled "Hey, want a burger?" to them from across the street. The larger one shouted back, "WHAT?" in an angry, unsettling way. He led the way, storming across the road, as the smaller one followed close behind. I had become quite accustomed to encounters of many kinds on the streets and

I don't spook easily. Before heading out on the streets, we always prayed, declared and believed in God's *zone* of protection.

Junior, the ironic name of the big guy, looked at me with a deep rage in his eyes and asked, "Do you want to die?"

The knife he flashed told me that this was a real threat. It was confirmed by Ryan (the smaller guy) who warned me, "He'll do it. He just bit the nipple off a stripper!" (Another "we didn't take this at Bible College" moment as Brian would say.)

Part of me froze, the other part of me, however, confidently knew that the spiritual world was more real than the physical one. These two men had a date with God that did not include me getting stabbed over a hamburger.

I knew that I didn't want to die so I threw in some humour and in one of my higher pitched, character voices I asked, "Do you want a burger?"

Despite the seriousness of the scenario, I watched as the seemingly ridiculous question travelled through Junior's chemically altered mind until it reached a still cognitive pocket.

"Uhhhh, yeah actually!" he said putting away the knife.

I took them inside and introduced them to our team and got them both a juicy burger. I caught Brian's eye and got him to run interference (one of our street strategies) on Junior.

After the crisis had been averted, God opened up the floodgates on Ryan. I quickly instigated a discussion with Ryan because it was clear something was going to happen, and the two gentlemen needed some distance to avoid distraction.

My friend Eric and I listened to Ryan's life story that began pouring out of him, without even asking. The most important detail was that he was running from a God he had heard about, but didn't think was actually real, alive, or interactive.

We could hear Junior inside getting ready to burst in on us at any time, so we asked if we could pray that God do *SOMETHING* right there and then for Ryan. He agreed to the experiment in a "I guess it couldn't hurt" way. We took a risk and asked God if He could sober Ryan up right on the spot, so he could physically FEEL Him.

We prayed what Pete Greig masterfully describes in "The Vision" as a "feeble, whispered, faithless prayer that invokes a thunderous, resounding, bone-shaking great 'Amen!' from countless angels, from heroes of the faith, from Christ himself."

Ryan physically jumped backwards saying that he felt something like a shock. He found himself sober and stunned. We knew our time was very short as Junior couldn't be distracted for much longer. So we prayed one more time that Ryan would wake up in the morning *KNOWING* that God was real in a very personal way. Immediately after that, Junior tore out of Freedom House like the Tasmanian Devil, grabbing Ryan by the arm and hurrying away down the street into the night.

I tracked Ryan down on Facebook when I got home and emailed him the question, "So when you woke up, how did you know God was real?"

By mid-morning he responded, "I just wanted to say thank you for taking the time to talk to me last night. It got pretty bad after we left, and I have a weird feeling today. I'll be where ya'll were last night on Sunday at 10:30 if that's where you go. I'm not a huge believer, but after the things that happened after myself and that guy left and waking up safe today with this strange feeling over me, makes me want to find something to put faith in. It just feels like the right time."

As it turns out, Junior stabbed and almost killed a man shortly after our encounter. It was a person that Ryan was planning on going after as well. Ryan came to church that Sunday morning and gave his life to Jesus.

JOHN'S STORY

John was a regular at Flippin' Fridays. He came almost every week. It wasn't long before he found out that Freedom House people were safe to talk to, so he began to share some of the struggles he was going through which included drugs and alcohol. You didn't have to talk to John very long to recognize what a great guy he was, but that he was losing his battle with these issues.

After a couple of months of building relationship and encouragement, John made the decision to follow God and we were able to help him find a substance abuse program where he went and lived for a few months to find freedom from these issues as well.

ROXANNE IS SILENCED BY THE HOLY SPIRIT

Roxanne showed up to Flippin' Friday very angry one night. We don't know why but it was very clear that she had some church background that wasn't favourable. She was mad at God, she was mad at the world and she was mad at us. She was talking fast and getting louder. The agitation in her voice and body language was becoming evident. I watched from a distance as she continued her animated conversation with a group of our ladies, and after 10 minutes I decided to run interference to ensure our ladies were safe and had an out if they needed it.

Roxanne was in the middle of explaining her various beefs with the church when I stuck myself into the middle of the conversation. Sadly, her story was all too familiar, and I empathized with the pain she must be feeling.

"Well that sounds really challenging," I responded.

My presence seemed to give her new boldness as she continued her angry rant with matter-of-fact accusations and venom. It was evident the pain and anger had been with her for a long time.

She was getting faster and louder.

"Roxanne," I interjected, "What do you want from us tonight?"

"Well, you're a church, right?" she asked.

"Yes, we..." and before I could finish.

"Well I don't believe in the church and I don't like the church. I don't believe in God. The church never does anything good."

"How's your hamburger, Roxanne?", I asked.

"It's really good"

"So, the church can do something good then, right?" and I smirked.

She smirked just a little.

"Roxanne, now that you believe that the church can do something good, what if I could prove to you that God exists?"

She looked interested, yet skeptical, so I kept going.

"Would it be ok if I had a couple of our ladies pray with you?"

"Sure, that can't hurt I guess."

I asked two of our ladies to pray for Roxanne and I knew that something was happening almost immediately because she stopped talking. It got quiet for about 10 seconds and then Roxanne blurted out "Holy S%#T, what was that?"

I explained to Roxanne that what she felt was God and He did this sometimes to prove that He's around.

Well, that was Friday night. Two days later was *Baptism in the Square*. Roxanne showed up, gave her life to Jesus and got baptized that day and threw in a few more expletives along the way.

IMPORTANT NOTE: Moments like these may cause some in the church to disregard the deeper things that God is doing. It is clear that he doesn't seem to get as easily offended as we do.

DON'T HIT HIM, HE'S THE CHEF

It was just after 2am on one of our first Flippin' Friday's. I remember that because one of our new interns spent a good portion of the night inside the building a little too freaked out to come outside. (Before the summers ended, she began to see what God was up to and the role that Christians can plan in bringing positive change on the streets. She became one of our best volunteers and champions of Flippin' Friday's.)

A few minutes later we were about to start cleaning up the BBQ when a huge commotion came from the bar across the road. We watched as one guy ran out of the bar followed by five other guys chasing him. Within seconds the one guy was surrounded by the other five.

It didn't look good and I thought to myself, someone should really step in and stop that before something really bad happens. Apparently that *someone* was me.

By now, all six guys were in the middle of the street. I pushed my way into the midst of the whole thing and tried to talk some sense into the situation. Nobody was listening. The guy by himself was probably the mouthiest of them all. It was very clear that the other five had plans to mess this guy up, and since he wasn't smart enough to shut up himself, I grabbed him by the collar, tightened my grip a bit and then positioned myself between the him and his five enemies.

It seemed like a good idea at the time, but all it did was anger the other five guys. One of them was right up in my face making threats to me. He was yelling and cursing and making very inappropriate gestures when all of a sudden, the guy farthest away yelled to him.

"Hey man, don't hit him, he's the cook."

The man stopped swearing at me. He stared at me, then he looked back at his friend who said, "Don't hit him, he's the chef."

He looked up at me again and said, 'Hey, you're the chef!"

My first thought was, 'I'm not sure I would call what we do at Flippin' Fridays chef-worthy' but instead of saying that out loud I simply responded, "Yup, I'm the chef."

The fact that the chef got into the middle of the fight was enough for them all to back down and cooler heads prevailed.

We talked through this with our volunteers after the incident. We are constantly amazed at how God invites us to get involved in the middle of many very interesting situations, but that He always protects us in the midst of it.

FLIPPIN' FRIDAY WRAP UP

We have shared just a few of our stories with you. As we have mentioned, we have met thousands of people over the last few years at our free BBQs. We have built relationship and mutual respect with most of them.

Some come because they are hungry, some come because they are lonely, some come to talk, some aren't sure why they come; but they are all people that God loves and those He has wonderful plans for. We continue to choose to show up and let God show off.

It really is remarkable what a simple BBQ has been able to accomplish over a long period of time.

We call it the *power of the burger*.

FREEDOM GATE APARTMENTS - AFFORDABLE HOUSING FOR THOSE IN NEED

After only a few of years in the bar, we realized we were outgrowing the space and needed a new home for Freedom House.

We started looking around the city for appropriate locations for our church and ministry center. A couple of guys that went to our church worked for a local businessman who owned quite a bit of property in the city. They told me of another bar that he owned that we might be interested in, so the next week I went to see that place.

After walking through the bar with them I realized it could be a great location for us and got the owners name and number from them. The owners name was Gabriel Kirchberger and I called him the next day.

Gabriel met me outside of our church the following day promptly at 10 AM. We walked through the building and in less than 10 minutes we were standing in front of our building again.

He said to me, "Brian, we could work out some kind of deal. We could trade buildings, or I could buy your building. But, I think your building is perfect for the affordable housing projects that are happening in the city. I think that's what you should do with this building."

And then he said, "I'll help you do it."

Just for the record, allow me to restate that I had known Gabriel for 10 minutes by this point and he's offered to help me transition our building from an ugly old bar into a new apartment building.

The next meeting with Gabriel included much of his staff at his office. I found myself sitting around his large board room table with Gabriel, his administrative assistant, his lawyer, his engineer and a few other staff members.

Gabriel introduced me as the Pastor of Freedom House church, with disclaimer that it was ok to work with me because "Brian doesn't think like a pastor". They agreed to work with us in transforming our church into an affordable housing complex.

The first thing they did was to help us apply for government grants. Our application was successful, and we received $750,000, specifically because of our partnership with him as a developer. From there, they interfaced with all the city officials and contractors to do the renovations on our building.

Within a couple of years, all the renovations were done, and we held the open house of our brand-new apartment building that we named Freedom Gate Apartments – a complex with 15 one and two-bedroom apartments.

God provided this unique partnership with a local business that has provided both for us, and for the residents of downtown Brantford. We couldn't have imagined a better way.

It was at this point in our history that Freedom House relocated to the very mall my wife Sharlyss had been accosted in, 20 years earlier.

KINDNESS PROJECT CONCERT SERIES

We were approached by several local business people asking if they could host some concerts for us. They said that they would do the bookings with the artists, they would book the venue (which was the largest theatre in our city) and they would take all the risk. All they wanted to do is give us the proceeds at the end of the day for all the money that came in from the concert.

It didn't take long to pray that one through.

Through the years they hosted several very successful concerts with the Canadian rock legends *Lighthouse*, *Bruce Cockburn*, and *Randy Bachman*. Each concert made between $15,000 and $20,000 which they gave directly to us allowing us to keep doing the things in the community that we are known for.

FROSTY FEST - BRANTFORD'S WINTER CARNIVAL

The story of Frosty Fest is shared in the previous chapter. I just want to add a couple of thoughts here, under the Kindness banner.

Firstly, we were approached to help run a winter carnival out of an established relationship and responding to the felt needs of the city.

Secondly, our city was actively pursuing the revitalization of the downtown which was the very thing God called us to do. Creating a new culture in our downtown that was hospitable and kind, especially for families to experience, was bringing the culture of heaven to our city. Frosty Fest has become one of the major events that has significantly changed the atmosphere of our downtown core.

Finally, we are often asked, "how do you do a winter carnival?" and our answer is always the same. Don't do one... unless the city needs one and

God has said to do one. The time, effort and resources needed to do a winter carnival are way more than you want to expend. With this said, however, it is very likely that God will highlight a need in your city that you think will take more time, effort and resource than you want to expend – that may be the thing that *YOU* need to do.

'SUPERHERO IN ME' KINDNESS CURRICULUM

We had experienced some success in getting Captain Kindness in the schools through assemblies that we had created. While these were great one-time events for the schools, we were hoping to make more of a lasting impact on the students' lives. Our children's pastor, Nicki Straza is a very talented writer who has written curriculum for a number of different groups. We brainstormed for a couple of weeks at our staff meetings with her and then released her to write.

What she came up with is a class curriculum called "Superhero in Me". It consists of eight workshops that take the students through an understanding that there is something of great value in them that can be expressed through kindness towards themselves, in their home, in their school and their community.

"Superhero in Me" has met with tremendous response and we are presently working on getting it into every school in our city and preparing training, so it can be exported to other cities as well.

KINDNESS CENTRE

The Kindness Centre is the name we gave to our ministry centre which takes care of the practical needs in our city.

It is a place where we can partner with other local groups and agencies that have similar vision.

It is a location where we do workshops for budgeting, food safety and job skills.

It includes a thrift store where families can come and shop in a dignified, respectful setting. All of the items are priced extremely reasonably. If, however, the price is too much, there are systems in place to be able to allocate free items for those in need.

It has also become a distribution centre for our local food bank.

The Kindness Centre is here to serve those in need and to help create volunteer opportunities for people inside and outside of Freedom House. Often clients will be become volunteers because of how much it has helped them.

THE KINDEST PEOPLE IN THE CITY

It is our contention that Christians should be the kindest people in their cities. We're not suggesting that non-Christians can't be kind, but since kindness is one of the fruit of the Spirit in Galatians 5, it would seem clear that we should have a head start in the kindness department. The reality is, when we bring our best to the table, God does as well. His favour, plus our kindness turns even our small feeble efforts into something that makes a difference.

As you can tell, none of the things we do under the banner of the Kindness Project are very technical or tricky. They are intentionally simple acts of kindness done *continuously* in our city to show the people here that they are loved.

In fact, we often joke around saying that our Kindness Project is what our grand-parents used to call "being a good neighbour."

The concept is not new. The Bible records the *no-strings attached kindness* of a Samaritan that has become international news ever since it happened.

Luke 10:25-37 On one occasion an expert in the law stood up to test Jesus. "Teacher," he asked, "what must I do to inherit eternal life?" [26]"What is written in the Law?" he replied. "How do you read it?" [27]He answered: " 'Love the Lord your God with all your heart and with all your soul and with all your strength and with all your mind'; and, 'Love your neighbour as yourself.'" [28]"You have answered correctly," Jesus replied. "Do this and you will live." [29]But he wanted to justify himself, so he asked Jesus, "And who is my neighbour?" [30]In reply Jesus said: "A man was going down from Jerusalem to Jericho, when he fell into the hands of robbers. They stripped him of his clothes, beat him and went away, leaving him half dead. [31]A priest happened to be going down the same road, and when he saw the man, he passed by on the other side. [32]So too, a Levite, when he came to the place and saw him, passed by on the other side. [33]But a Samaritan, as he traveled, came where the man was; and when he saw him, he took pity on him. [34]He went to him and bandaged his wounds, pouring on oil and wine. Then he put the man on his own donkey, took him to an inn and took care of him. ³⁵The next day he took out two silver coins and gave them to the innkeeper. 'Look after him,' he said, 'and when I return, I will reimburse you for any extra expense you may have.' ³⁶"Which of these three do you think was a neighbour to the man who fell into the hands of robbers?" ³⁷The expert in the law replied, "The one who had mercy on him." Jesus told him, "Go and do likewise."

There are a couple of interesting points to note here.

Firstly, Jesus told this story as a follow up to the discussion he was having about the great commandment which is to love the Lord your God with your heart, soul, mind and strength AND to love your neighbour as yourself. Given that these are the most important commands according to Jesus, which he then connects with acts of kindness, we should be hearing what he is saying and obeying.

Also, it is noteworthy that these acts of kindness done by the good Samaritan were done without expectation of anything in return. It was totally given with no-strings attached.

Let me state this very clearly one more time for the record; we should be the kindest people in our cities. We should be known for our kindness because it is the character of the living God who resides in us. We should do these acts of kindness and live our lives full of kindness with *no-strings attached*.

WHY KINDNESS?

Kindness is needed in our cities.

As the world grows more and more apart, there is a greater need for intentional activities and opportunities for us to come together. Kindness can be both the magnet and the glue in these circumstances.

Not only is it needed, but KINDNESS WORKS! (Don't miss the double meaning here that kindness itself works and that there is work involved in kindness.)

Ecclesiastes 11:6 (TLB) says, *"Keep on sowing your seed, for you never know which will grow—perhaps it all will."*

Sometimes we see immediate results, and much is done by faith; trusting God with the results, but we know that kindness works. Because of God's character and His word, we are expecting that every seed of kindness that is sown is going to produce a harvest.

We have seen how small acts of kindness over long periods of time can change any individual, any neighbourhood or even an entire city.

Kindness is working for us and it will work for you as well.

9

ONECHURCH - PARTICIPATING IN THE TRANSFORMATION OF THE CITY

It had been almost a decade since Celebration 2000, the first of three disruptions in our attempt at intentional city-wide transformation.

The chairman of the Pastors' Network had retired from his church and subsequently withdrew himself from leading the network. I was approached by a couple of the other pastors on the team to see if I would let my name stand in a vote to choose a new chairman. I explained that I still desired to see a unified network who worked together for city transformation and they assured me that this was the same desire they had. So, with some trepidation I put my name in and was voted in as the new chairman for the Brantford Evangelical Ministerial Association.

The core leaders of the network began to meet regularly for the next year. We agreed that we would be very intentional about prioritizing relationship and establishing a strong foundation of unity in our understanding of who we were and what God wanted to do in our city.

We changed the name of the group from the Brantford Evangelical Ministerial Association, to ONEchurch taken from our desire to honour Ephesians 4 together.

Ephesians 4:1-6 says, *As a prisoner for the Lord, then, I urge you to live a life worthy of the calling you have received.* [2] *Be completely humble and gentle; be patient, bearing with one another in love.*[3] *Make every effort to keep the unity of the*

Spirit through the bond of peace. ⁴There is one body and one Spirit, just as you were called to one hope when you were called; ⁵one Lord, one faith, one baptism; ⁶one God and Father of all, who is over all and through all and in all.

As we walked through those first few months, we established that God had brought us together to be unified as *THE CHURCH* in Brantford. From this came our Mission Statement: "ONEchurch, participating in the transformation of the city." It was our desire to bless each other and see transformation in our city.

While we recognized our calling as Pastors to be *spiritual gatekeepers* in the city, we chose to partner with others who were participants in transformation as well. We were careful to acknowledge other *gatekeepers* in the areas of business, education and government who were also foundational in our pursuit of city-wide transformation. We agreed that there was a significant need to collaborate with those in other spheres of influence. This included those inside and outside of the church.

THEOLOGICAL FOUNDATIONS

Early on, we were very intentional about choosing theological foundation for our group. ONEchurch would be built on common truths that we could all agree upon rather than doctrines that have historically divided the church. We agreed on the Apostles Creed, the Great Commission, and the Great Commandment.

Apostles Creed
I believe in God the Father, Almighty,
Maker of heaven and earth:
And in Jesus Christ, his only begotten Son, our Lord:
Who was conceived by the Holy Ghost,
born of the Virgin Mary:
Suffered under Pontius Pilate; was crucified, dead and buried: He descended into hell:
The third day he rose again from the dead:
He ascended into heaven, and sits at the right hand of God the Father Almighty:
From thence he shall come to judge the quick and the dead:
I believe in the Holy Ghost:

I believe in the holy catholic church: the communion of saints:
The forgiveness of sins:
The resurrection of the body:
And the life everlasting,
Amen.

Great Commission

Matthew 28:18-20 says, *Then Jesus came to them and said, "All authority in heaven and on earth has been given to me. [19]Therefore go and make disciples of all nations, baptizing them in the name of the Father and of the Son and of the Holy Spirit, [20]and teaching them to obey everything I have commanded you. And surely, I am with you always, to the very end of the age."*

Great Commandment

Luke 10:27 He answered, "Love the Lord your God with all your heart and with all your soul and with all your strength and with all your mind; and, Love your neighbor as yourself."

These were the tenants of faith we agreed upon, forming the theological framework for church unity and service to our city.

COMMITMENT TO EACH OTHER

After getting through these initial points, we started to discuss some more specific issues. How were we doing as *one church*? We used the example of Christ's letters to the seven churches in the book of Revelation as our framework. It was clear from reading the first three chapters of Revelation that Jesus had some approval and some critique for the churches.

I asked the group this question: "If Jesus wrote a letter to the church in Brantford what would he say? What would he commend us for? What would he challenge us to do differently?"

We walked through this dialogue with honour and respect, coming away with some clear points on how to work together. It was very exciting.

Those who would connect to ONEchurch would do so understanding the commitment we have made to each other and to the city. We are committed:

- To the vision and mission of ONEchurch to *"participate in the transformation of the city."*

- To each other, believing that relational unity comes before philosophical unity, which comes before functional unity.
- To a culture of honour and unity – not allowing known division to exist.
- Individually as Pastors, and to teaching our congregations about unity and transformation. We would engage our congregations to participate together with ONEchurch initiatives, so that together we could really be *one church for the city*.

As previously discussed in chapter 3, we had learned a few lessons about unity and specifically the need to have relational, philosophical and function unity - in that order.

Even with our challenging history and some of the mistakes of the past, we recognized our responsibility to the city and each other and chose to act on both of these. We agreed that the Lord still had great plans for our city and made the choice to work together in unity to see His will come to pass.

INVITE THE MAYOR

With these foundations in place, we were ready to take further steps in blessing our city.

I developed a relationship with our Mayor through several other intentional and random meetings. I told the ONEchurch Executive that when we were ready to work to bless the city, that I would set up a meeting with him to get his input on where the city-wide church could best be a blessing.

We invited our Mayor for a lunch meeting with our executive to discuss how ONEchurch could serve the city. He was encouraged to see the church reaching out and agreed to the meeting.

After a couple of meetings with the executive he agreed to speak at one of our monthly luncheons with the broader ONEchurch network. At that meeting, he listed a number of issues in the city. However, the issue dearest to his heart at that time was the need to ensure that every child in our city had good nutritious meals every day at school.

The Mayor left the luncheon and those who stayed behind agreed that we would immediately start a Task Force to help meet this need in our city. We started meeting together as the Task Force, networking with others in the city working on this same issue. We continue to grow in our influence and impact in providing meals for students.

We were aware that there were many other needs in the schools but agreed that we would start with what our Mayor had asked. We kept the bigger picture in mind of how to eventually reach all the spheres of influence, while starting where we were invited to take part.

COMMUNITY ACTION TEAM

It wasn't long before other issues were coming to our attention and it was very exciting watching those in our churches bringing thoughts and ideas to us. It was becoming clear that people were recognizing the church role in solving societal issues.

We progressed from the food programs to actually adopting schools. We committed to pray for them and to offer to meet practical needs whenever possible.

Our next intentional step was to recruit people from all areas of society to be involved in the team. We have been very proactive in the integration of people from varied callings and professions coming together for the sake of the city. We presently have sub-teams of the Community Action Team released to work on Business, Education and Government. While this is happening, the Pastors are working together on making sure our families and churches are strong. We see this outflowing of the *Ekklesia* as a direct answer to Jesus' statement that he would build his church (Matthew 16).

We continue to work hard at obliterating the sacred and secular divide that can exist in the church. We have seen the positive results of leveling the playing field in what used to be the clergy and the laity, with intentional dialogue about the importance that everyone fulfills their callings as part of the *Ekklesia*. Our choice to engage people from various spheres of influence has released many across the city to rise up with passion and expertise to bless our city.

UNITY, UNITY, UNITY

We have talked about unity already in this book, but I want to break down our understanding a bit further to really grasp both the layers and the process of developing effective unity.

Level One – Family/Relational Unity

Firstly, we need the unity of family. Even though we may be part of different churches, we are part of the same family. Take time to truly get to know other Pastors and marketplace leaders in your city. Find out what they are passionate about and what God has placed on their heart for the city. Without this, when challenges come, or doctrinal differences arise, the automatic reaction will be to separate back into our own little places in the Kingdom. However, when there is relationship built, we have a foundation to build on. Once the other leaders in the city are your friends, you will want to work together, and separation will not be an option.

Understanding that family unity is a deep level of relational unity is significant, and I use the two terms synonymously in this book. Our commitment to relationship, as the family of God, must be the bedrock of unity in our city.

Level Two – Philosophical Unity

Secondly, we need philosophical unity. Once we've chosen to do life together and work together for the sake of the city, we need to agree on "HOW" we will move forward. For us in Brantford, this philosophical process took about a year to establish and remains an ongoing dialogue. We discussed extensively God's desires for the city and how we would partner together to pastor the city, instead of just our individual churches. We re-branded the city-wide pastor's network to ONEchurch using Ephesian 4 as our primary unity chapter declaring that in Brantford, there is "ONE Lord, ONE faith, ONE baptism" and ONE Church.

Level Three – Functional Unity

Once we had worked towards family and philosophical unity, then we proceeded with the third phase which is functional unity. This is the phase where we intentionally chose to work together serving the city, believing that we are much better together than apart. It's not that our individual churches hadn't been active in the city, but we had not worked together since those dreaded days of Celebration 2000.

Now, ONEChurch functions together in several ways.

We meet weekly for prayer, monthly for lunch and numerous other times throughout the year.

We have yearly events on our calendar including: The Civic Prayer Breakfast; the Canada Day park clean up; Leadership Development days; among others.

Both our ONEchurch executive and the ONEchurch Community Action Teams meet monthly to ensure ongoing vision and momentum. Sub-groups of the Community Action Team meet as is necessary to keep moving forward in our desire to *participate in the transformation of the city*.

In conclusion, the development of effective unity can be summarized as follows:

- We made a commitment to each other (Family/Relational unity).
- We made a commitment to specific, core biblical truths and how to express them with honour (Philosophical unity).
- We made a commitment to the city; to act as one and participate together as one church in the city (Functional unity).

Since we set this process in place, we have both maintained relationships and increased our involvement and influence in the city.

The Church - the *Ekklesia* - should be a *go to* organization for the city when they need a group that will work and serve with no-strings attached.

We are grateful to God for what He is doing and excited for all He is going to do in and through us as we continue to foster our relationships with him and each other.

ONECHURCH EKKLESIA CHAMPIONS

The following list represents our present leaders in ONEChurch, both the executive and the Community Action Team. Participating in the transformation of the city includes many committed individuals who deserve honour and thanks.

Bruce Mann

Bruce is a leader of leaders that can a bring a group of people together like no other. He is a man of integrity who is thoughtful and wise.

Bruce and Wanda (his wife) have sown into this community for almost 30 years. Bruce is the chair of our ONEchurch Community Action Team.

Craig McKibbon

Craig is the Pastor of Evangel church in Brantford. He is very passionate about our city.

For several years now, Craig has been the Chaplain of our local police department. Serving our first responders in such a way deserves huge honour.

Craig is a great guy, even if he is a rabid Patriots fan.

Terry Cioni

Terry is the Pastor of Pleasant Valley Church.

He moved here with his young family several years ago, stepping into a very challenging scenario the first day he arrived. He walked this challenging path with much grace and fortitude.

Terry is a Pastor's Pastor who loves this community and has served faithfully where others may have stumbled.

He has some of the best *one-liners* and delivers them masterfully.

Greg Pulham

Greg is the Pastor of Freedom Christian Community.

Greg has lived in Brantford most of his life. He pursued a legal career for several years and then felt the Lord call him to change ministry focus.

Greg's desire to see God's Kingdom expanded here in Brantford has been exemplary. He has been willing to ask the hard questions of church growth and community service.

If you ever need someone to take minutes at a meeting, Greg should be a strong consideration, he loves to do it.

Lance Tweedy

Lance is the Pastor of Celebration Church.

Lance transitioned the church his father planted almost 30 years ago with honour and integrity.

He is passionate and creative in finding ways to serve the city.

He is the most genuinely happy person you will ever meet. #HappyChurch

Ralph Byma

Ralph has been the Pastor of Grand Valley Christian Centre for over 20 years. He is also the president of Elim Canada.

Grand Valley has served some of the neediest families in our city for years. They have done so with an unwavering expectation of God's goodness to overwhelm our city.

Years ago, God gave Ralph a prophetic picture of how there would be a group of leaders rise up in Brantford that would work together in unity and see the glory of God displayed here in a historic measure.

I believe that we are seeing some of that now and that we are on the very brink of seeing total fulfillment of this prophetic word.

Fausto Victorio

Fausto is creative innovator, who presently owns and runs *RCITY Co-working Space*.

He is a member of the ONEchurch Community Action Team who consistently brings strategic thoughts and insight to our group.

Fausto is always looking for ways to expand God's Kingdom *Ekklesia* in our city.

Susan Zuidema

Susan is a passionate mother and community leader. She is deeply concerned for families and the education field.

She is a skilled communicator who keeps our city-wide church family in the know of everything that is happening.

David De Dominicis

David is a Real Estate Agent who has a strong calling to see the city transformed.

He recognizes his calling to minister in the business sphere and sees it as a significant way to bring the Kingdom of God to our community.

David's strong family and community roots are a significant strength to our city-wide team.

His mom makes some of the best spaghetti sauce you will ever have.

Dave Carrol

Dave is a strategic, big-picture thinker who brings both insight and foresight to our city-wide team.

He is an exceptional communicator and is one of the most creative people you will ever meet. He can weave his way through dialogue about church, politics and business without skipping a beat.

It's been said that Dave looks a lot like Captain Kindness. I can neither confirm nor deny this however, I can tell you that I have never seen the two of them in the same room together.

ONECHURCH – PARTICIPATING IN THE TRANSFORMATION OF THE CITY

Our ONEchurch network continues to grow in both depth and scope. The desire to see *all the church, take all the gospel, to all the city* only comes through these intentional sacrificial relationships.

10

THE GOSPEL OF THE KINGDOM

God is zealous to see His Kingdom expanding in our cities. Jesus came as the one who was going to establish a Kingdom that would be ever increasing and never ending. That is important for us to understand as we are partnering with God to bring His *Kingdom on earth as it is in heaven*. In order to do this, it is imperative that we have a Biblical, Kingdom worldview, which simply means that we see everything through the lens of the Kingdom of God.

In 800 BC, the prophet Isaiah made some very exciting declarations about the coming Messiah - who he would be and what he would do.

Isaiah 9:6-7 (NKJV) For unto us a Child is born, unto us a Son is given; And the government will be upon His shoulder. And His name will be called Wonderful, Counselor, Mighty God, Everlasting Father, Prince of Peace. ⁷Of the increase of His government and peace there will be no end, upon the throne of David and over His Kingdom, to order it and establish it with judgment and justice from that time forward, even forever. The zeal of the Lord of hosts will perform this.

That child was Jesus.

Even the most superficial overview of the gospels will unveil this significant understanding. Jesus came to establish the Kingdom. He told parables about the Kingdom. The Kingdom of heaven is *like this*; the Kingdom of God is *like that*. It was clear that he wanted his listeners, both then and now, to understand that there is a King, with a Kingdom and a plan to get his ever-increasing, never-ending Kingdom here.

He emphasized this most greatly, when he gave us his pattern of prayer found in Matthew 6.

Matthew 6:7-13 (NKJV) And when you pray, do not use vain repetitions as the heathen do. For they think that they will be heard for their many words. [8]"Therefore do not be like them. For your Father knows the things you have need of before you ask Him. [9]In this manner, therefore, pray: Our Father in heaven, hallowed be Your name. [10]Your Kingdom come, Your will be done on earth as it is in heaven. [11]Give us this day our daily bread. [12]And forgive us our debts, as we forgive our debtors. [13]And do not lead us into temptation, but, deliver us from the evil one. For Yours is the Kingdom and the power and the glory forever. Amen.

We often repeat this prayer by memory which is wonderful, but I am concerned that we get tragically close to the *vain repetitions* that Jesus warns us about before he gave us this model. Look at that again. We're not to use *vain repetitions*, expecting our Father in Heaven to hear us because we have said so much. Rather, we are to pray, then believe, then act.

"YOUR KINGDOM COME, YOUR WILL BE DONE."

What if Jesus actually meant that?

What if He really wants His Kingdom to come on the earth as it is in heaven?

What would it look like if God's will, was actually done in our cities?

Most likely one of the first things that would need to happen for His Kingdom to come and His will be done, would be for our kingdoms and wills to be moved aside. Too often, our personal dreams and plans can be in conflict with God's dreams and plans. Sometimes we are guilty of doing stuff we were never called to do, asking God for provision for objectives he never gave us vision for in the first place. It has always *been* about His Kingdom and always *will be* about His Kingdom.

One of Christ's final statements about the Kingdom of God comes later in Matthew's gospel. In Matthew 24:14 Jesus says, *"And this gospel of the Kingdom will be preached in the whole world as a testimony to all nations, and then the end will come".*

What does that mean?

What is the *gospel of the Kingdom?*

We know that gospel means "good news", and we know that Kingdom means "the king's domain or place of rulership". So, the "gospel of the Kingdom" is the good news that the king reigns and rules in our lives and cities.

However, much of the North American church has limited this rulership to the spiritual realm, where we have allowed Jesus to come and save our souls. We have embraced the gospel of salvation, the good news that Jesus saves our souls; over the gospel of the Kingdom, the good news that Jesus wants His Kingdom to come to every aspect of our cities.

It would be our contention, that the gospel of salvation is *contained* in the gospel of the Kingdom, remembering, it is the gospel of the Kingdom that will be preached in all the world prior to the Lord's return in Matthew 24.

Perhaps this next point will help clarify further. In the garden, God created a perfect place for Adam and Eve to dwell in unison and relationship with Him. When they sinned, they initiated a death process that would affect both them and us. A process that will stay in effect until God reverses it in eternity. That death process includes our whole being; spirit, soul and body. Adam and Eve lost everything good that their Heavenly Father had given, but the promise was that one day, a second Adam would reverse the curse and take back everything that was lost by the initial act of sin.

So, what does that include?

RECLAIMING EVERYTHING THAT WAS LOST

All Christians would agree that Jesus came to provide salvation for us. He came to reverse the consequences of sin, (eternal separation from God) by redeeming us from the curse of the law through his death and resurrection. Jesus is our Saviour! Jesus saves! Amen.

Many Christians would also agree that Jesus' redemptive plan covers every area of our lives; spirit, soul and body. Jesus wants us to live free in all of these areas. Much has been written of late regarding *sozo*[1], the Greek word for salvation which means to save, heal, preserve, and make completely whole. Jesus completely saves and redeems us, *Spirit, Soul and Body*, and provides abundant life now, not just in eternity.

These great results of Jesus' life and work for us, bring us back to

Genesis 3 and solve our sin problem, which is amazing. With this said, I would suggest that believing in these two provisions is still only accepting the *gospel of salvation*. I believe Jesus wants to take us further and His life mission was in fact, to help us grasp what He called the *gospel of the Kingdom*.

The Gospel of Kingdom takes us all the way back to Genesis 1:1 *"in the beginning God created"*. It is here that we have a divine invitation to partner with the creative nature of God, to bring His solutions to every area of our cities. Now, to be clear, this is not "create" as in, *let's go speak and see stars and planets appear*; but rather, *let's get creative to bring answers to the challenges in our physical world that He originally created*.

Since we have been created in God's creative image (Gen 1:27), we have an invitation and a mandate to bring transformation to all of creation, not just to solve the problem of personal sin found in Genesis 3.

Transformation, therefore, includes the significant impact of what happens everywhere in our cities, not just the consequences of sin from the fall of man.

Every significant transformational leader that I know, affirms this understanding.

Ed Silvoso, in his book *Transformation* affirms the same when he reminds us of Christ's' conversation with Zacchaeus recorded in Luke 19. And Jesus said to him, *"Today salvation has come to this house, because he also is a son of Abraham; for the Son of Man has come to seek and to save that which was lost"* (Luke 19:7,8). Silvoso points out that Jesus came to *seek* and save *that which was lost* which including Zacchaeus' life, his family and his work.[2]

Dr. Myles Munroe, author of Rediscovering the Kingdom says, *"We're finally getting to the original message, the original assignment, and the original goal of God. It has always been the restoration of His Kingdom on earth. It is the only message Jesus preached that we can verify. God is restoring the original message of the Bible. This is very significant. It's important to note that Jesus placed the end of the age on the condition that the message of the Kingdom is preached into all the world. I went to college and have a degree in theology, but there was not one class on the Kingdom. I read the four Gospels and it was the only thing that Jesus preached. That was a very strange contradiction to me. The Spirit of God has been speaking about the Kingdom for years, but we are finally listening and that's exciting to me. We will see the true impact of the Kingdom if we keep preaching it."*[3]

Bill Johnson writes, *"In redeeming man, Jesus retrieved what man had given away. From the throne of triumph, he declared, 'all authority has been given to me in Heaven and on earth. Go therefore...'. In other words: I got it all back. Now go use it to reclaim mankind. In this passage Jesus fulfils the promise he had made to his disciples when he said, 'I will give you the keys to the Kingdom of Heaven'. The original plan was never aborted; it was fully realized once and for all in the resurrection and ascension of Jesus. We were then to be completely restored to his plan of ruling as a people made in His image. And as such we would learn how to enforce the victory obtained at Calvary: 'The God of peace will soon crush Satan under your feet'.*[4]

Oz Hillman writes, "In order to go beyond the Gospel of Salvation to the Gospel of the Kingdom we must exercise a different level of faith for our communities. Jesus talked about the kingdom of God more than 70 times in the New Testament – much more often than he mentioned salvation. While salvation is part of bringing the kingdom of God on earth, it includes much more. When the Gospel of the Kingdom comes into a life and a community, everything in its wake is transformed."[5]

Chuck Colson, in his book *How Now Shall We Live* writes, "*The church's singular failure in recent decades has been the failure to see Christianity as a life system, or worldview, that governs every area of our existence.*"[6] Because the gospel of the Kingdom is the good news of the rule and reign of the King, this has to include both the people and the affairs of the Kingdom. Therefore, a Christian after being saved, needs to continue to live under the sovereign rule of Jesus in his personal life, with his family, and in the marketplace.

This is where the local church comes in; to disciple and equip its members to discover and fulfill their calling; releasing each one into ministry towards fulfilling the great commission. Consequently, this will produce an extended Church that reaches out and influences the world, and *not* a nuclear Church where God's power and influence is confined within the walls of a building. This is the *Ekklesia*.

WHAT DOES THE KINGDOM LOOK LIKE?

We can clearly see; most transformational thinkers and writers have agreed that we need to have a broader view of society. Various authors have suggested their own analogies for this creative, kingdom process. They all include the integration, rather than the separation of the church and the marketplace.

These areas of society have been described as, "spheres of influence", "domains", "gates", or "mountains". To me, the name is inconsequential. The most important piece is understanding the need to intentionally raise up and release Christians into their field of interest, passion, and expertise.

I was first introduced to this approach through the writings of Loren Cunningham in his book *Making Jesus Lord:*

"Sometimes God does something dramatic to get our attention. That's what happened to me in 1975. My family and I were enjoying the peace and quiet of a borrowed cabin in the Colorado Rockies. I was stretched out on a lounge chair in the midday warmth, praying and thinking. I was considering how we Christians - not just the mission I was part of, but all of us - could turn the world around for Jesus. "A list came to my mind: categories of society which I believed we should focus on in order to turn nations around to God. I wrote them down and stuck the paper in my pocket. "The next day, I met with a dear brother, the leader of Campus Crusade for Christ, Dr. Bill Bright. He shared with me something God had given him - several areas to concentrate on to turn the nations back to God! They were the same areas, with different wording here and there, that were written on the page in my pocket. I took it out and showed Bill and we shook our heads in amazement. Here's a list (refined and clarified a bit over the years) that God gave me that sunny day in Colorado: 1 The home; 2 The church; 3 Schools; 4 Government and politics; 5 The media; 6 Arts, entertainment, and sports; 7 Commerce, science, and technology."[7]

I find this story particularly fascinating because of both the undeniable divine inception and the resulting global impact.

ALL THE CHURCH, WITH ALL THE GOSPEL, TO ALL THE CITY

Whether you call them *mountains*, *gates*, *domains*, or *spheres*, the bottom line is we believe and expect every area of our city to experience transformation. By encouraging our people to take His Kingdom to work wherever that may be, we release *all the church with all the gospel to all the city*.

For the record, you won't find a *chapter and verse* of 7 Mountains or spheres in the Bible, if you are so inclined. What you will find is overwhelming evidence that we are to be "salt and light" and that everything we set our hand to should be done as unto the Lord. We use the terms "mountains" or "spheres of influences" interchangeably in our ONEchurch network in Brantford with the following list:

1. Arts and Entertainment
2. Church (or religion)
3. Business
4. Education
5. Family
6. Government
7. Media

I particularly like how this list fits with the ultimate glory that Jesus deserves as found in Revelation 5.

Revelation 5:11-12 Then I looked and heard the voice of many angels, numbering thousands upon thousands, and ten thousand times ten thousand. They encircled the throne and the living creatures and the elders. ¹²In a loud voice they sang: "Worthy is the Lamb, who was slain, to receive power and wealth and wisdom and strength and honour and glory and praise!"

Consider this:
Arts and Entertainment - *worthy is the Lamb to receive* **glory**
Business - *worthy is the Lamb to receive* **wealth**
Church - *worthy is the Lamb to receive* **praise**
Education - *worthy is the Lamb to receive* **wisdom**
Family - *worthy is the Lamb to receive* **honour**
Government - *worthy is the Lamb to receive* **strength**
Media - *worthy is the Lamb to receive* **power**

ARTS AND ENTERTAINMENT

...*worthy is the Lamb to receive glory* (Rev 5:12)

If ever there was a mountain that the end result was glory, the entertainment industry would be it. Glory, applause, accolades, plus a lot of money are at the end of this rainbow for the successful individual.

Do we need proof that this sphere is influential? One word - *Hollywood*! The amount of influence that Hollywood has is staggering. They have the ability to capture our thoughts, imaginations and hearts, areas where God wants to be pre-eminent.

Arts and entertainment encompass many areas of lives, including art, music, theatre, sports, fashion, movies, dance, and every other way that people celebrate and enjoy life.

The good news is our Creative God is looking for those in His image to rise up in creativity and imagination to be key leaders in this arena. He is seeking and finding "artsy" and "sporty" people to bring Kingdom traits to this hugely influential industry.

Pete Greig helps us with his thoughts. *"Does God speak by His Spirit through our creativity? Bezalel was filled with the spirit of God, with skill, ability and knowledge in all kinds of crafts and his call was to decorate the prayer room (Ex 35:30 – 34). In the same way today, God has given creative leadership to those who have His Spirit. While some will use His creativity for idolatrous purposes, we shouldn't be diverted from our proper use of it because of any form of guilt by association. No wonder we are beginning to see contemporary Christian artists: poets, painters and rock stars filled with God's Spirit, influencing the broader culture as did Handel and Michelangelo."*[8]

God is releasing music, art, poetry, drama, and every other creative medium from Heaven to Earth.

Lord, let your Kingdom come.

BUSINESS

...worthy is the Lamb to receive wealth (Rev 5:12)

Business creates wealth. The bible tells us that it is the Lord who gives us the ability to create wealth and that we should always remember this.[9]

Until recently, the popular teaching within the church was one which exalted poverty over wealth. By doing so, we allowed the *Spirit of Mammon* to control the economy of the planet. After all, "money is the root of all evil" is it not? Actually, Jesus' teaching was that the love of money was the root of all evil and then he went on and taught more about money and economic principles that any other subject. In fact, the Bible is filled with writings on wealth and prosperity.

Our jobs, abilities, witty ideas and skills are God given. Business leaders and entrepreneurs bring a mindset to the church and to the

Kingdom that is vital if we are to lead the way in innovation and creativity.

Earlier in this book, we looked at God's desire to prosper us as we enter into a *hear God and obey* relationship with Him. The promise was, *"if you are careful to obey everything, I have told you, I (God) will make you prosperous and successful."*

The truth is, that in North America prosperity is not a spiritual right, it is already a responsibility. Having realized this, however, we must come to an understanding of prosperity that is biblically sound.

Our definition of prosperity became, "prosperity is having everything you need, to do everything God calls you to do." We believe this is a definition that is both Biblically accurate (knowing that God will give us everything we need for life and Godliness -1 Peter 4:1); and that it also transcends geography (which means this definition works in the 3rd world as well as the 1st world.)

The idea of Biblical prosperity has become controversial but cannot be ignored if we want to see His Kingdom come on earth as it is in heaven.

Christians need to go after the sphere of wealth with a vengeance. Both the need to honour those called to business and the immense need for Kingdom finance, demands it. To accomplish what God is saying for us to accomplish in this hour, necessitates it.

God is looking for business people and entrepreneurs with integrity that he can partner with to bring wealth to His Kingdom for the sake of Kingdom purposes.

CHURCH / RELIGION

... worthy is the Lamb to receive praise (Rev 5:12)

Our highest calling as a Christian is to worship the Lord. It is intimacy with God that brings us into the place of knowing our Heavenly Father, knowing His heart, knowing our calling, and knowing His power.

Unfortunately, when the church models a Christianity that does not carry power, presence and passion, then we are demonstrating a product that's so inferior that many other counterfeits can thrive. Taking the mountain of religion and worship is an awesome assignment, but it is still the heart of the Father that all people might know His great love.

God has set eternity in the hearts of men and each person is on a quest to respond to that calling. The church will need to be free to walk in our high calling with confidence and compassion.

Ephesians 1:17-23 I keep asking that the God of our Lord Jesus Christ, the glorious Father, may give you the Spirit of wisdom and revelation, so that you may know him better. [18]I pray also that the eyes of your heart may be enlightened in order that you may know the hope to which he has called you, the riches of his glorious inheritance in the saints, [19]and his incomparably great power for us who believe. That power is like the working of his mighty strength, [20]which he exerted in Christ when he raised him from the dead and seated him at his right hand in the heavenly realms, [21]far above all rule and authority, power and dominion, and every title that can be given, not only in the present age but also in the one to come. [22]And God placed all things under his feet and appointed him to be head over everything for the church, [23]which is his body, the fullness of him who fills everything in every way.

God wants to give us wisdom and revelation to know what to do and how to do it on every occasion. He wants to open our spiritual eyes to see:

- Who He is "to know Him better" (vs 17)
- Our Hope (vs 18)
- Our Inheritance (vs 18)
- His Power which is available to us (vs 19)

Spirituality is at a premium today and it is our responsibility to display the glory of His Kingdom everywhere we go in a powerful and protective way.

EDUCATION

...worthy is the Lamb to receive wisdom (Rev 5:12)

Education is the system where thoughts become mindsets and ideologies become lifestyles. The biblical decree to train up a child in the way they should go has never been more important or challenged as it is today.

Schools and universities that originally began as training for higher education, often to educate developing clergy, are now the stronghold of liberal thoughts and ideologies. Many of our places of learning have entered into a philosophy that displaces God from the centre and puts man there instead.

Bill Bright states:

"In America, influential educators have taken God out of our textbooks. They teach evolution and deny the biblical view of creation. Moral relativism is destroying our young people. Advising them to do 'whatever feels good'. These educators deny God's authority by contending that values are relative to the individual and the situation."[10]

We need Kingdom-minded teachers from preschool to university; people of God rising up in their calling to influence the sphere of education. Educators need to be released into every system of learning with Holy Spirit power, authority, and love.

FAMILY

...worthy is the Lamb to receive honour (Rev. 5:12)

Genesis 2:18, 22-24 The LORD God said, "It is not good for the man to be alone. I will make a helper suitable for him." [22]Then the LORD God made a woman from the rib he had taken out of the man, and he brought her to the man. [23]The man said, "This is now bone of my bones and flesh of my flesh; she shall be called 'woman,' for she was taken out of man." [24]For this reason, a man will leave his father and mother and be united to his wife, and they will become one flesh.

The family is the first institution that God created. It was His idea from the beginning that a man and woman would come together to create a family. As such the family is also the foundation and fabric of our society. The family was designed to be a place of safety, love, encouragement, discipline, respect, and change. It is the first environment that an individual will experience the tension of fighting for valuable relationship.

The fact that the family unit is being attacked on every side is not surprising, but it is not acceptable to sit back and allow this onslaught.

Malachi 4: 5-6 (NKJV) Behold, I will send you Elijah the prophet before the coming of the great and dreadful day of the Lord.[6]And he will turn the hearts of the fathers to the children, and the hearts of the children to their fathers, lest I come and strike the earth with a curse.

We should expect, believe and fight for this *heart turning* in our day and time. Those who understand the *Gospel of the Kingdom* are uniquely qualified to demonstrate God's original purpose for families. When our families are intentionally forged in love and respect, the natural outflow is for this type of relationship to spill into other areas of society as well.

Strong cities come from strong families.

GOVERNMENT

...worthy is the Lamb to receive strength (Rev 5:12)

Romans 13:1 Everyone must submit himself to the governing authorities, for there is no authority except that which God has established. The authorities that exist have been established by God.

1 Timothy 2:1-4 I urge, then, first of all, that petitions, prayers, intercession and thanksgiving be made for all people— ²for kings and all those in authority, that we may live peaceful and quiet lives in all godliness and holiness. ³This is good, and pleases God our Saviour, ⁴who wants all people to be saved and to come to a knowledge of the truth.

All authority has been given by God and there is no sphere of influence that this is more important than the mountain of government. For too long, the argument of the division between church and state has kept many Christians out of this arena.

I write about this in length in Chapter 12, The Myth of Church and State Separation.

The revelation of the Kingdom is bringing life and hope to many who have felt called to politics, but have not known how to respond. God is calling and releasing His people today into this mountain and they will position themselves in places of authority for the sake of the Kingdom and its mandates.

MEDIA

...worthy is the Lamb to receive power (Rev 5:12)

Media in this context refers to outlets that report and establish the news. This includes TV stations and networks, computers and websites, newspapers, radio stations and magazines. They have power to report and at times actually create the news by what they focus on.

Presently, most media sources are extremely Liberal. When big business owns the media, or lobbyists pay off those in the media, how objective is the information?

Dick Staub, in his book The Culturally Savvy Christian asserts, *"People who believe they know the truth need to realize that cultural influence requires more than knowing the story, it requires telling the story thoughtfully and artistically. Never has there been a greater need for wise, gifted storytellers who understand the story we are in and can communicate a better way truthfully and gracefully."*[11]

It is clear that we need Holy Spirit-led communicators and storytellers in our world today. Since the "Kingdom of God is righteousness, peace and joy"[12], these media artists must learn how to creatively infuse every news outlet with the good news of the Kingdom.

If "knowledge is power", then whoever controls the knowledge has the power. The *Lamb of God is worthy to receive all power,* making it imperative that Kingdom-minded Christians be committed to this sphere of media.

SACRED/SECULAR DIVIDE

The news of God bringing revelation to be intentionally involved in these mountains is very exciting. Neither the simplistic, nor strategic nature of this message can be overstated. The majority of the body of Christ is *out there* in the workplace. The problem is we have not taught them how to enjoy the presence and power of God in their jobs.

Part of the challenge to this point has been the sacred/secular dichotomy that has permeated our North American church thinking. The error has been that we have exalted certain callings and jobs, over others.

Bluntly stated, we have elevated Pastoral or church related vocations as sacred and placed them over every other calling - perpetuating the division between the clergy and the laity.

This, in turn, has caused most Christians to consider their *secular* employment as just a job and not a calling. Often, this brings both guilt and shame to these Christians for not being involved in more *sacred* endeavours.

But what about the young man who obeyed God by becoming a lawyer or a teacher?

What about the woman who knew she had heard the voice of God when she said "yes" to becoming a doctor or a business person?

Are we really going to stick with the argument that sometimes obeying God is holy, yet other times obedience is *less than holy*? That sometimes obeying God is sacred and other times it is not?

This whole mind-set, which really is a spiritual stronghold, is a poor understanding of the way God created us. It is left over Greek philosophy that we inherited from our European ancestors. It is rooted in the Gnostic view that part of our lives, (the spiritual part) is separated unto God; but the rest of our lives (the physical part) is not. This is the dichotomy of the sacred and secular.

The way we should think is found in our Jewish roots, which confirms that all of our lives are holy and set apart for the Lord. Which, if played out in the above context again, proves that whatever God says is holy – is holy. Therefore, whatever God calls and equips a person to do is also holy.

THE MANDATE OF THE KINGDOM

The following are poignant words of wisdom by Howard Snyder that bring us back to a Kingdom world-view.

"The church gets in trouble whenever it thinks it is in the church business rather than the Kingdom business. In the church business, people are concerned with church activities, religious behaviour and spiritual things.

In the Kingdom business, people are concerned with Kingdom activities, all human behaviour and everything God has made, visible and invisible. Church people think about how to get people into the church; Kingdom people think about how to get the church into the world. Church people worry that the world might change the church; Kingdom people work to see the church change the world.

We have heard for years the discussion about the 80/20 principle. This is the commonly quoted ratio often referred to as ratio of people who do ministry within the church – 20% of the people do 80% of the ministry. It has been a reference point for the average leader – "How can we get more people involved in the church? Maybe we have been asking the wrong question." [13]

If the advancement of the Kingdom of God is the goal, then being strategically active in every sphere of society or mountain is a necessity. Therefore, when we have strategically encouraged and empowered our people to influence these other mountains with excellence and integrity, in reality we have increased our ratio dramatically. Ultimately, to the place where 100% of our people see their lives as ministry (not just the Pastors).

Beyond this, releasing the entire church to their vocations with a divine sense of Kingdom-calling, heightens both our understanding and expectation of what God wants to do in that area where we spend the majority of our time and energy. We love to encourage our people to stop "working for the weekend" and having a passion for Mondays as much as Sundays. We call it a *TGIM* or *Thank God it's Monday* attitude.

I understand in writing this chapter that I am going to challenge most thoughts on why we do church and why the church exists, and I'm ok with that. I had to chew on this information myself for a while. As Lester Sumrall once said, "One of the disturbing things about Christianity is that very few Christians ever advance beyond their first revelation."

The best I can do now is to suggest you go back and read the gospels again and highlight every time Jesus talks about the Kingdom of God. I believe that will bring another level of revelation on this subject.

We would all agree that we want to see God's ever-increasing, never-ending Kingdom in our communities.

I'm going to let Loren Cunningham conclude this chapter.

Cunningham says, "Jesus has commanded us to go and disciple all nations. In the past we have gone into countries as missionaries, giving the gospel and teaching the people how to read and write. We didn't get involved in teaching government, politics or economics. We let the Marxists do that. In country after country in the Third World, the Communists took young men educated in missionary schools and 'discipled them on how to run a government'. As we disciple the nations by giving them godly economic systems, Bible-based forms of government, education anchored in God's Word, families with Jesus at the head, entertainment that portrays God in His variety and excitement, media that is based on communicating the truth in love, and churches that serve as sending stations for missionaries into all areas of society, we will see the fulfillment of the Great Commission and multiplied millions coming into the Kingdom of God. Jesus promises that as we do this, 'I am with you always, even to the end of the age' (Matthew 28:20).[14]

Lord, let your Kingdom come and your will be done in our cities as it is in heaven.

11

THE CULTURE OF THE KINGDOM

God's Kingdom has a culture, and our role as Christians is to make our culture looks as much like Kingdom culture, as possible.

Culture has been defined as, "The sum of attitudes, customs, and beliefs that distinguishes one group of people from another. *Culture* is transmitted, through language, material objects, ritual, institutions, and art, from one generation to the next".[1]

What are the beliefs, customs and attitudes of the Kingdom of God and how should this Kingdom be portrayed in comparison or contrast to our culture?

CANADIAN CULTURE

I am Canadian. Canadian culture is known for a few things:

We're nice.

We're peace keepers.

We're sarcastic (we got that from the British).

We're not very confrontational.

Most Canadians suffer from what I call a "low grade insecurity", but we like to call it humility. Unfortunately, we have allowed this to stop us from dreaming big or believing that God could do anything really big in Canada.

Some of these qualities are good and some not so good. Clearly this is not an exhaustive list.

Combine this with the fact that we have a very liberal and secular culture and we are faced with a Kingdom challenge. But, whether good or not so good, my Canadian culture has to be brought to the cross to get heaven's culture.

Now think about your culture, how close is it to the culture of heaven?

CHURCH CULTURE (NORTH AMERICAN)

The church in North America has a bad reputation.

If you google "Christians are" you will have further evidence of how those around us see the church and you will not be happy about what you find. My Google search found that Christians are hypocrites, ignorant, losers, haters and those that lead them (preachers) just want your money.

I can't imagine how this represents the culture of the Kingdom of God.

The church in North America doesn't look much like the church Jesus came to establish, as portrayed in the New Testament. The North American church could be accurately described in the following ways.

- It is more attractional than it is incarnational.
- It is more inward focused than it is outward focused.
- It is way more concerned with information, than transformation.

These factors have brought us to the place where we are ignored, irrelevant, or worse. Most Christians leaders who are objectively analyzing the church culture in North America are justifiably concerned.

We need to bring our *church culture* to the cross as well. We need to find out what Jesus meant for His church to be and replicate that today.

What did Jesus have in mind when He created the church?

What did He want it to look like?

What did He want us to look like?

The great news is that we don't have to guess about this. Jesus was very specific about this whole discussion.

KINGDOM CULTURE

We don't use the term *Kingdom* very often. Because of that, it will be important to define what a Kingdom is and also be able to recognize some of the components of a Kingdom.

Literally, a Kingdom is a "king's domain." It is the place where a king rules and reigns.

Next, we need to understand that there is a king in a Kingdom. More specifically, in God's Kingdom there is a king – and you're not him. There's only one King in the Kingdom of God.

Also, a Kingdom has territory. It is the expanse of the Kingdom. According to Isaiah 6, God's Kingdom was meant to be *ever increasing and never ending*.

Kingdoms have citizens. Presently, that's us, but God's desire is that this would be everyone, since he is not willing that any should perish (2 Peter 3:9).

Lastly, Kingdoms have a culture; a system of beliefs, values and attitudes that is transmitted through language, rituals and institutions.

As we previously discussed, the understanding of gospel of the Kingdom is paramount to transformational thinking. God's desire is that His rule and reign extend into every sphere of society through His character and values.

Our national cultures and our church cultures have to bow to the culture of the Kingdom of God.

JESUS BUILDS HIS CHURCH

Jesus said "I will build my church" as recorded in Matthew 16:18.

Jesus intentionally chose the word He used here. The word we translate as church is *Ekklesia*. *Ekklesia* is a Greek word which means "called out."

In Greece, *Ekklesia* was a term used for those Greeks that were selected, "called out", then trained up to know the best about the Greek culture and live and lead this culture by example. These were the best educated and the best leaders of their society. They were the decision makers, the influencers – much like our city councillors, business networks or neighbourhood associations would be today.

Ekklesia was a secular word that Jesus borrowed to describe what he was building. *Ekklesia* was always used to describe a group or gathering of people, never a building. Jesus did not use the two most religious options he had – temple and synagogue – He said He was building His *Ekklesia*.

Jesus could have used the word temple which was a place of worship that was understood by His disciples. Jesus could have said He was building a synagogue which was a place of study. But He did not use either of these terms, He used *Ekklesia* and when Jesus said this, his disciples were both shocked and excited at the same time.

Jesus was not building another building, He was going to build people that He would pour His Kingdom culture into, with the expectation that they would go and take His Kingdom everywhere they went.

KINGDOM CULTURAL ARCHITECTS

You've probably heard the phrase before that "the church is a hospital for the hurting and not a museum for the saints."

I would suggest that the church is not solely either of these things. The church, or *Ekklesia* is both of these things and much more. If you are hurting you should be able to come to the church and get healing, but to say that this defines the church, limits what the *Ekklesia* really is.

The more we try to compartmentalize what we think the church is, the further we get away from what Jesus meant when He said that *He would build His church*.

A museum is a place you go to check out what has happened before in history. From the visit, hopefully you can learn from the good, so you can repeat it and learn from the bad, so you can avoid it.

The Bible also describes the church with several different analogies. The church is an army, which excites those who see themselves as Holy Spirit warriors, but that is not the total picture of the church. The church is also a bride, a spiritual house, a family, and several other things.

When we go after one analogy of what the church is at the expense of other analogies, we limit what Jesus said He was building.

All of these analogies are crucial to our understanding of God's desire to influence and transform all areas of in our cities.

We must remain true to the words of Jesus who said that His church was an *Ekklesia*. The church is people - transformed people who would transform all of society.

How much of the city should get transformed?

The answer is everything, which is the understanding that Jesus had when He said that He would build His *Ekklesia*. It is a Kingdom-minded "city council" that would bring heaven on earth. They are leaders and influencers that recognize their calling and anointing within every sphere of society.

The *Ekklesia* is Kingdom people – cultural architects - bringing creative, Kingdom solutions to the city, so systematic poverty becomes systematic prosperity. It is part of the fulfillment of the Isaiah 6 mandate to see God's Kingdom *ever increasing, never ending, everywhere*.

As we bring our national cultures and church cultures into alignment with the culture of the Kingdom of God we are transformed and empowered to that Kingdom transformation everywhere we go. Transformed people, transforming society.

The *Ekklesia* is me.

The *Ekklesia* is you.

Be encouraged to find your place and fulfil your role in it.

Lord, let your Kingdom come and your will be done on earth as it is in heaven.

12

THE MYTH OF CHURCH AND STATE SEPARATION

"Give us, dear Lord, the good grace to work for, what we pray for."
- Sir Thomas Moore

I love this prayer from Sir Thomas Moore. I love it because it talks about the need for both work *and* prayer. I also love it because it is our Mayor's favourite prayer.

That's right. You read that correctly; it's our Mayor's favourite prayer.

Is he allowed to have a favourite prayer? If he is, is he allowed to say it publicly? What about the separation of church and state?

WHAT IS IT?

What is the separation of church and state?

Is it the government NOT interfering with what is happening in religion?

Is it religion, NOT running the state?

Is it the expectation that there is a great wall between church and state and *never the twain shall meet?*

I believe that most people would have a problem if the state tried to dictate what we had to believe in the realm of our faith, or demand that we couldn't believe at all. Furthermore, I think it is reasonable to say that most would agree that religion cannot push their beliefs on those running the government. But, besides these two extremes, I think there is a significant vacuum of real knowledge as to what the phrase "separation of church and state" really implies.

It is not my intention to do a deep dive into the history on this point, except to recognize that most people know the phrase, but have no idea what it really means. Because of this, it would seem that we have had an *"us vs. them"* relationship, specifically regarding how the church relates to government and vice versa.

This is the challenge that I want to address in this chapter. We have heard for years from a few detractors in our city that Freedom House shouldn't be allowed to do our events on the public spaces because of the *separation of church and state*. It seemed like all the loud voices were saying we couldn't do things in public places. To be honest, even some of our friends in both the church and governmental realms were a little concerned.

But, I want to tell you that it's all a farce – it's a myth.

Church and state can and should work together to see that the city and our people are blessed and can live hope-filled, prosperous lives.

Several years ago, we hosted the North American Transform Our World Conference in Brantford. By chance, our MP Phil McColeman (Member of Parliament) was also hosting The Honourable Jason Kenny who was the Minister of National Defense at the time. He agreed to address the crowd for a brief speech and gave the most eloquent delivery of how the government welcomed the church to step up and take an active role in our communities. He ended with the phrase "the church is not just wanted, but needed in our society," which, as you can imagine, was met with thunderous applause.

BECOMING KNOWN FOR BEING "FOR" NOT "AGAINST"

Perhaps one of the reasons why churches experience push back from the political leaders in their cities is how we have projected ourselves over the years. Too often, we have gone to our governmental leaders expecting them to act on our behalf, when doing so, has put them in very uncomfortable situations.

A chat with a city Mayor over a decade ago confirmed that premise. He told me that a certain church group had invited him to come and join them for an event, giving him a great seat on the platform, front and centre. Their service included some statements about the city and expectations that weren't spelled out before the event. He mentioned that he felt like they had him on the platform to convince the audience that he was in agreement with everything they were doing – which he clearly wasn't. He said it made him want to turn down all future events connected with any church group.

I wish that I could say that this was an isolated incident, but it is not. Pastors and spiritual leaders have acted disrespectfully for years, which has led to some of the church vs state separation. Some have led with negative attitudes and judgmental spirits, afterwards expecting their city leaders to respond favourably to their requests.

The opposite is also true, I have heard from many pastors and leaders that have tried to connect with their Mayors or ward councillors, but have had no affirming response.

Perhaps both sides should try to see that we are actually working for the same goals. The main goal is to see a healthy prosperous city. Is it possible that it would be to our mutual benefit to learn to work together as much as possible?

The church could take the lead on this and become known for what we are *for* in our cities over what we are *against*. Maybe combine this with an understanding from Christians that *if we want to have influence, we need to have involvement.* If we are aware of the church and state tension, it would be wise for us to take some time to build relationships with those in our city, serve their vision for a while before we expect anything from them.

We stumbled across this more by the grace of God rather than own brilliant intellects. Much of this came from our involvement with the city as we were converting our first building from a church into affordable housing. The project warranted that we take very specific, step-by-step actions and we observed the supportive responses that we received from those in the positions of authority in the city. There wasn't even mention of the fact that we were a church. We decided that we wanted to help meet a need in the city. City officials wanted to see the same needs met and we bonded over helping those in our community. Any *church vs state* tension that may have been there was alleviated over time as we worked together for a common, positive goal.

PASTOR THE CITY

Transformational thinking comes with a broader context than most can wrap their heads around. For example, one of the first realizations that come is that you are called to *pastor the city*, not just your individual congregation.

That's why if you ever ask me how many people are in my church, I will usually answer 120,000.

I can take you to the exact location in our city when God spoke this to me. I was driving to the south end of our city. As I sat at the stop-light on the corner of Brant Ave and Colborne Street I clearly heard God say, "I want you to Pastor the city". When I first heard it, I wasn't even sure what it meant. To be honest, I am still coming to understand the full revelation of the phrase.

What I do know is that His desire is that His love and kindness would be shown everywhere in our cities and that He is asking us to partner with Him to make sure this happens.

The other great truth that comes from this, is the acceleration of the need to work for the integration of all the spheres of influence in our cities. When the entire city is the goal, even the least astute person will acknowledge that no single person, or church could accomplish that goal. When pushed a little further we see that we really do need business, education, government and the *Ekklesia* working together for significant transformation to occur.

A POLITICAL RUN, A HORRIBLE DEFEAT, A BIGGER WIN

I know a little about the political arena from my short run for public office.

It was 2008 and our boys, Renyck and Brayden had just gone back to school for the fall. During this time, they were deciding if they should run for class president, vice president and one of the other positions. I told them both that I thought that they each had leadership potential and that because of such abilities, they should offer those abilities to the school and see what would happen.

When I said that to my boys, I realized that I should take my own advice and offer my leadership to the city and run for city council. My words to my boys became my own personal challenge to go beyond what I had been taught in Bible college regarding what you are supposed to do as a *typical Pastor*. I had to work through what it meant for me to actually *Pastor a city*. So, I ran for city council and I lost horribly. It wasn't even close.

What came from those few short months in the political race, however, has provided insight and wisdom right up to the present. The people I met, the debates I participated in, and the discussions I had after the debates, began relationships and collaborations that proved to be very rewarding. I gained a completely new understanding and appreciation for those that serve their city in the realm of government.

MUNICIPAL, PROVINCIAL AND FEDERAL GOVERNMENT IN UNITY

While discussing how church and state should function well together, I would be remiss if I didn't acknowledge three significant political leaders who were in office concurrently in our city for many years. They are Mayor Chris Friel, MPP Dave Levac and MP Phil McColeman. For years these men worked tirelessly to participate in the transformation of our city. I know from working with each of them, the number of selfless hours they spent to see our city become a provincial and national leader again. They have done so by working together in amazing unity for the sake of our city, even though they come from varied political parties. They have led by example in this.

I honour you, Chris, Dave and Phil for your efforts and I consider it a privilege to call each of you a dear friend.

LOW J-COUNT OR HIGH J-COUNT EVENT

Over the years, we have had to learn how to manage both church and state expectations when it comes to being involved in public events in the city.

We came to the understanding that we needed to evaluate our events prior to responding to invitations or booking public spaces, to determine if they were a *low J-count or high J-count event*.

A *low J-count* event means a *low Jesus-count* in public. For example, Frosty Fest is a low *J-count event*. We understand that we are partnering with the city to put on a great family weekend. Out of respect, we will not be publicly vocal about our faith. We have no problem with this. We understand boundaries and agree to them up front.

We also have *high J-count* events. *Baptism in the Square* is a *high Jesus-count* event that we run in Harmony Square. We go through the proper channels to rent the space and pay for all the extra equipment needed, just like any other city group would do. With that done, we then set up our band, have a great worship time, preach the gospel and graciously welcome new people to come and experience God in a public space.

Some anti-church protagonists in the city never want to see the church in public, no matter what the reason and regardless of whether we have gone through the right channels. Some Christians in the city are concerned that we have watered down the gospel by hosting or being involved in events where the name of Jesus is not repeatedly declared from the stage. We take no issue to either thought process, but neither do we agree with them.

The truth is, even in the *low J-count events* there is still a *high J-count* because we are the *Ekklesia* and we bring the presence of Jesus wherever we go. This understanding is paramount for those wishing to participate in the transformation of their cities.

We have found that we can trust the power of the Holy Spirit to work through us all the time, even if we can't use the type of church language that some wish we could.

For us, making and following clear boundaries, with large doses of respect and honour have been a winning combination in the church and state discussion in our city. We expect that it will work for you as well.

POLICE BOOTS FOR JAIL RELEASES

Several years ago, we received a call from one of local police officers, Jim Sawkins. Jim has a huge heart for our city and was looking for a way to give back to our community. After thinking through it, he came up with the idea of getting our local police force to donate their boots to the Kindness Centre for those in our city who needed good boots. He called his program "Sawkins Boots."

He told us that because the officers receive a yearly stipend to buy new boots, often the used ones are still in good shape when they purchase new ones. He asked if we would be able to give them away. We assured him that we could. So, once or twice a year, we receive a delivery of 2 or 3 large boxes of amazing boots from our police department.

Here's where this gets fun. We also had an agreement with the chaplain of our local jail, that any men getting out of jail could come by the Kindness Centre to get a new outfit upon release.

We found great joy and humour in the fact that there were numbers of recently released convicts, walking around our city, wearing former police footwear.

HOCKEY NIGHT IN BRANTFORD, WITH A TWIST

Brantford is a hockey town with the greatest hockey player of all time, Wayne Gretzky being from our city.

Our MP, Phil McColeman is a huge hockey fan. He loves to watch, and he was a great player in his day as well.

For years he had wanted to do an event called *Hockey Night in Brantford.* Some of the other MPs from our province were hosting these celebrity hockey games and so I was chosen as one of a group of guys from Phil's leadership team to go check out the game in Barrie, Ontario. We came back and shared with the rest of Phil's team that we thought it would be a great community event.

The concept was a simple celebrity hockey game, with local hockey players from the past and those who were currently playing in the NHL. The purpose was to raise money for a local charity and that was a wonderful incentive to get involved as well.

After working with Phil on his re-election as our MP, I volunteered to be the chair for Hockey Night in Brantford to get it up and running. We already had a great team from the election, so I knew that we could pull off this new venture.

We worked hard for eight months and we were getting down to the wire, with only about a week to go before the big event.

This is where the story gets really amazing.

The last week leading up to *Hockey Night* was one of the busiest of my life. Not only did we have all the last-minute details to do for the hockey game, but the Sunday just before, was set to be our first *Baptism in the Square*. We had taken a full-page ad out in our major newspaper and we were expecting a huge crowd to show up that Sunday. Monday was scheduled for a three-hour meeting for *Hockey Night* and then Thursday would be the actual hockey game.

The Sunday came, and it was a beautiful sunny, warm day in Brantford. We had no idea who would show up for *Baptism in the Square,* but we were believing for a great crowd. When I arrived in Harmony Square, I was amazed at how many people had come. Our church had done a remarkable job praying and believing and God did not disappoint us.

The worship team was ushered in the presence of the Lord, God anointed His word as I spoke and by the end of the event, almost one hundred people had come forward for salvation and to get baptized in the public square. We were ecstatic to say the least.

As I mentioned, we had bought a huge ad in our local paper, but we didn't send a specific press release for them to come and cover the event. But, they sent a reporter anyways. I remembered seeing them there when we baptized the first person in line. I thought to myself that this was a really nice gesture on their part and to be honest I didn't think much more of it. The next day, I started to get phone calls from people in my church.

"Have you seen the Expositor today?".

"Did you get a copy of the paper yet?"

Well, not only did they get a shot of the first baptism, it covered the whole front page of the paper with the caption, *"Baptism Attracts Hundreds to Harmony Square."*

How amazing is that? There's not a chance you could miss it! Everyone will see that!

Everyone, including all the people that were coming to the last *Hockey Night in Brantford* meeting. That included our Member of Parliament and his staff, our Fire Chief, our Police Chief, numerous other influential business people, plus a bunch of other city workers.

So, to recap; Sunday was *Baptism in the Square*, Monday I have become "John the Baptist"(recognized all over the city because I'm on the front page of our major newspaper), Monday night we are heading to our MP's house for a three-hour meeting about a charity hockey game that is going to take place on the upcoming Thursday.

Dave Carrol was with me and I said to him, "I don't know what God is up to, but I hope it's something good."

We walked into Phil's house and after a few pleasantries, I opened the *Hockey Night in Brantford* meeting up for discussion. It was one on the greatest meetings I have ever had in my life. We talked about hockey for about thirty minutes, then we talked about God for about three hours. Three hours with some of the most influential people in our city. They kept asking amazing question, after amazing question; about us and Freedom House and God. There was not a cynic in the room. Just honest people who were wanting to ask honest questions about the most important decisions in life.

To this day I still have people bringing up that meeting, how significant it was for them and how it had pointed many of them back to God. That *Hockey Night in Brantford* planning meeting has led to many, many, more very much like it.

We couldn't have scripted that night any better if we had tried.

Let me remind you that time spent building genuine relationships, living a real Christian life in front of people can turn a planned hockey meeting (low J-count) into an opportunity for the Holy Spirit (high J-count) to answer questions from honest seekers.

THE MAYOR'S COUCH CONVERSION

It was a Thursday night in early December, when my phone interrupted my reading. It was the Mayor on the line.

"I want to speak at Freedom House this Sunday", he said.

"Ok, Chris, sounds like a great idea. What's the occasion?" was my response.

"Well", he replied, "you're going to want to call it a conversion experience."

He had my attention. He kept talking about what had happened to him the night before at his home.

"I was sitting on my couch and I thought to myself, 'I'm going to be a Christian'. I was thinking about my Catholic roots and why my parents sent me to a Catholic High School. I was introduced to religion there for the first time - in fact, I played Jesus Christ in *Godspell* at that school. I had several conversion opportunities, but never responded.

"That's amazing, Chris" I replied.

He continued, "Actually, I always thought that if I became a Christian it would be like a Saul on the Road to Damascus experience. God would have to knock me off my horse for this to ever happen. But, I was just sitting on my couch and I decided - JESUS IS MY GUY - and I want to share my story at Freedom House."

After I reminded Chris that he didn't have a horse, I agreed that he could come and speak at Freedom House that Sunday, with great excitement.

Chris came to Freedom House and shared his story that Sunday. And our people laughed and cried and cheered and welcomed our Mayor into the family of God.

THE FREEDOM HOUSE 10TH ANNIVERSARY WEEKEND

Two months later was our Freedom House 10th anniversary weekend. On the Saturday we thought that we would host a casual, drop-in, media event. We did an open house for the afternoon and at a set time, we asked the local media outlets to come and hear some speeches from our local dignitaries and other guests.

At the appointed time, people were invited to come and share their thoughts about what Freedom House meant to them. It was all very touching, and the media took a bunch of pictures.

Then, our MP Phil McColeman took the mic and said some really lovely things about Freedom House and how much he appreciated us. And the media took some more pictures.

Next, our MPP Dave Levac spoke about the importance of people who step up and make their cities a better place. He thanked Freedom House for serving the city with passion for a decade. And the cameras clicked again.

Finally, it was Mayor Friel's turn.

He started with, "I only have one regret about Freedom House."

I wondered where he was going with this.

"I only wish that Freedom House had started 10 years sooner, because then we would have seen transformation in our city way before now."

How great is that?!

He continued, "And I love the way Freedom House worships."

And I wondered where he was going with this. We weren't having a worship night; it was a media event.

"Now, I'm not as comfortable as they are in displaying their worship way up here," (he raised his hands above his head). "I'm more of a hands down by my side kind of guy," (and he pulled his hands down again.) "However, I've been hanging out with a bunch of Filipino Catholics and they've helped me get my hands up to here," (he raised his hands about chest high.) "But, in honour of Freedom House's 10th Anniversary, I want you to take your neighbours hand and I want you to put it as high up in the air as you can, and I want you to repeat after me...'PRAISE YOU LORD, JESUS CHRIST, PRAISE YOU LORD, JESUS CHRIST, PRAISE YOU LORD, JESUS CHRIST'."

And our people cheered and laughed and cried and the media took lots and lots of pictures.

Separation of church and state? I think not.

13

OTHER CITY CHAMPIONS

Becoming the *Kindest City in Canada* isn't just about a specific church or even a group of churches (*ONEchurch*) working together, it is about a change of thinking and action from a broad spectrum of those in our city.

We have found that there are many people in our city who are very passionate about having a prosperous and thriving city as well. We have come to realize that city transformation is in the heart of God and it comes out of many people, in various ways.

At Freedom House we have been pursuing the transformation of our city, with the primary mode of outreach being kindness initiatives. We wanted to be actively involved in kindness, while celebrating and being a catalyst for others to do the same.

THE VOLLIES

Years ago, we decided that we would host a Freedom House appreciation night where we highlighted the amazing volunteerism of the people at our church. We set this night up like an awards show and called it 'The Vollies'.

After a couple of years of doing *The Vollies* for our Freedom Houser's only, we decided to add one award for a person outside Freedom House to honour someone in the community who embodied what Freedom House was trying to exemplify in our city. So, at *The Vollies* that year, we added an award called the *Honourary Freedom Houser Award*.

These are the stories of our *Honourary Freedom Houser's* over the years.

2012 HONOURARY FREEDOM HOUSER - GABRIEL KIRCHBERGER

Gabriel is a businessman of German descent who has been in Canada for about 25 years. He is a real estate investor, who buys, sells and managers many properties in Brantford and in other locations in North America and beyond.

Gabriel has a huge heart for our city, specifically the downtown. He had already bought and renovated a number of old buildings there, including the first of three buildings that would become the bordering buildings around Harmony Square. He eventually built, or rebuilt, all three.

As discussed in chapter 8, Gabriel is the gentleman that we worked with to transition our former church into affordable housing. He is also the one who made our present location very affordable (rent free) for over a decade.

Without reservation, I can say that for years, Gabriel Kirchberger was very significant in the success of Freedom House. His business expertise and generosity were instrumental in our continued growth and success. We will be forever grateful for his enormous investment into Freedom House.

I have also heard from numerous other charities, that Gabriel has been extremely generous with them as well. He doesn't talk about it much because that's not the type of person he is. However, I can say without a doubt that the transformation of our city could not have happened had Gabriel not seen the potential in an old, depressed city.

Both the Freedom House story and the story of the transformation of our city would be incomplete without Gabriel Kirchberger being honoured.

With the discussion of Gabriel and his company, G. K. York Management, I really need to acknowledge Gabriel's staff manager, Cathy Oden as well. Cathy is a wonderful Christian lady that loved everything that

Freedom House was doing in the city. She was a great advocate for us in several of the business networks in the city including the Chamber of Commerce, the Downtown Business Improvement association and of course, Gabriel's company.

God has an amazing way of having the right people in the right places for the right time.

2013 HONOURARY FREEDOM HOUSER - LORI-DAWN CAVIN

Lori-Dawn Cavin has been a tremendous part of the transformation of our city. Lori-Dawn works for the city as the Manager of Community Recreation Development for the Brantford Parks and Recreation. Although she works for the city, what she does for the city goes way beyond her 9 - 5 job. She has consistently worked to see that our city is one where its people want to stay and work, live and play. She epitomizes what it means to be a transformational leader.

Our collaboration with the city through our relationship with Lori-Dawn has included: Canada Day, Movies in the Square, Frosty Fest, Living Nativity, among others.

We have partnered together for more than a decade and I can honestly say that Lori-Dawn is one of the most hard-working, community champions in our city. Lori-Dawn embodies what every city worker should aspire to; in that, she clearly loves the city and exemplifies that love in a consistent and conscientious way.

Lori-Dawn gets how kindness can change a city and she lives it out like few others I know. We look forward to many more years working with her.

2014 HONOURARY FREEDOM HOUSER - LUCAS DUGUID

Lucas Duguid is an extraordinary man with a great story. He has been recognized numerous times in our city for his expertise in various fields of endeavor.

Lucas is one of the most passionate community advocates in our city. However, it wasn't always this way. Lucas would describe himself as a recovering cynic, with an unhealthy dose of apathy on the side.

Here's how he tells his own story:

"I came from this place of a great deal of cynicism and apathy my entire life up until that point.

I came downtown, very much into harm's way, in front of what I would later discover to be a church in the middle of the night – with people coming out of bars; people with mental health issues; some had addictions. Right in the middle of all of that were high-top tables, chairs and a BBQ and people from Freedom House are serving these people – they were serving everyone.

It took 3 or 4 visits, over several Flippin' Fridays for me to understand that this was truly service. There was no agenda. There was no angle. As much as I needed to find out why are they doing this, the answer was simple – service to community. How someone could not be inspired by that, shocks me.

I can point with a straight line and a ruler to that day; the moment I finally understood service to community through Freedom House Church and Flippin' Fridays. I can walk that line straight back to today - that's where my life was course-corrected in terms of my approach to community, my approach to volunteerism, my approach to my friends and family. Everything changed a little bit that day and I continue to be thankful.

Don't tell me – show me. You can tell me all day long, but when you show me, when I see with my eyes what it means to serve, when I see people stand up with their own resource, their own time and their own two hands to help - you can turn a non-believer into someone who is willing to walk in the light.

I was very much in the dark. Churches have an opportunity to show people like me that there is room for people like me. That I can have a place where I can help and I can be inspired by the action of churches to do that." – Lucas Duguid

In 2017, he was chosen as the Entrepreneur of the Year for the Brantford Chamber of Commerce. In 2012, the Downtown Business Association named him the Downtown Champion of the Year. Lucas continues to use entrepreneurial skills to assist many businesses and charities in our city to bring ongoing transformation.

I am honoured to call Lucas my friend and celebrate his passion, his perseverance and his overcoming spirit.

2015 HONOURARY FREEDOM HOUSER - BILL HARDING

I met Bill through our mutual love of the political arena. We worked on a campaign for our local MP Phil McColeman about twelve years ago and began to talk about our mutual desire to make our city great. We haven't stopped talking and working together for that end.

Bill has been a community advocate for many, many years in Brantford. More specifically, Bill has been very influential in advocating for local sports for young people in our city. He is presently the chair of the Brantford Sports Council which is a collaboration of organizations providing a collective voice for the ongoing education and promotion of the benefits of sports in the community.

During one of our meetings with Bill, he asked me, "What kind of Christians are you? Have you ever heard of *born-again* Christians?"

My reply was, "I don't know of any other kind, Bill".

I showed him the passage of scripture in John 3 where Jesus explained to Nicodemus that he needed to be *born-again* and why that was so important for our life now and for eternity. Bill agreed that day and said "yes" to Jesus.

Bill has helped us connect and collaborate with some of the finest people in the city. He has supported us in many of our ventures and volunteered at almost all of them.

I honour you, Bill. You are a great city advocate and transformation partner.

2016 HONOURARY FREEDOM HOUSER - GERRY BYRNE

Gerry Byrne is the manager of Thorpe's Funeral Home in Brantford. I met Gerry when I was performing a funeral for Thorpe's a few years ago. After the funeral I mentioned to Gerry that I would be willing to help him conduct funerals for families that wanted a spiritual component, but, didn't have a Pastoral connection.

Several months later, the Downtown Business Association was having our Annual General Business Meeting at Thorpe's and Gerry and I struck up another conversation. Between the funeral and the business meeting, Gerry had checked me and Freedom House out a bit.

We were only a couple of months away from Frosty Fest, our winter carnival and Gerry asked what he could do.

I told him that we were looking for a business to sponsor and run our snow slide that we would build on the edge of Harmony Square. He liked the idea, so Thorpe's Brothers Funeral Home became one of our key sponsors that year. Not only did they sponsor the event, Gerry brought key workers from his business over every day to help kids get up the ramp to slide down in what was one of the most bitterly cold Frosty Fests that we have ever had - all with the most amazing attitudes.

Now there are very few community events that we do that Thorpe's Brothers Funeral Home does not sponsor now. He's a yearly sponsor of Frosty Fest, Flippin' Fridays and our Kindness Centre Christmas Banquet.

One of his workers, Ed Crawford, became a regular volunteer at our sponsored school's breakfast program and eventually became our Santa Claus at our Christmas Banquets. He has one of the most amazing Santa costumes I have ever seen. There's a strong chance that he could be the real Santa.

I don't know anyone in the city that has a bigger heart than Gerry Byrne. He truly loves people and loves the city and he proves it with his actions.

2017 HONOURARY FREEDOM HOUSER - DANNY CAMPBELL

The Campbell Family are icons in our city. For over 45 years Campbell Amusements has been a provider of family entertainment throughout Ontario and Eastern Canada, with over 45 carnival rides and countless midway games. Don and Joyce Campbell started the business that their son Danny, together with his family, now leads.

We met Danny as we were preparing for the first year of Frosty Fest. His company owned an old-fashioned carousel ride that we felt would be perfect for our event. We negotiated and settled on the $5000 as our price. The event was a rousing success,

When we approached him the following year to discuss Frosty Fest he blew us away, not only by offering us five rides free of charge, but giving us 10% of the ticket sales.

The result of our negotiations for year three was even greater than we could have imagined.

Danny prefaced his generous offer by telling us "I have lived in Brantford all my life. I was raised here. I have wonderful memories here. I remember when our town was booming with prosperity and I remember when the recession hit and many people lost their jobs. I remember how the downtown used to be an exciting place to be and then how it became a bit of a ghost town because of lack of commerce. And, I have watched over the last few years how the downtown is coming back to life, and the role that Freedom House is playing in that story."

With this said, he offered to bring his 5 rides, his equipment, and his staff for FREE, and he said he was going to donate all of the proceeds of the event to Freedom House. The ongoing generosity of Campbell Amusement has enabled us to keep going through increased expenses and many changes through the years, investing in the long-term sustainability of Frosty Fest – Brantford's Winter Carnival.

There are few people who are city transformers, but the Campbell family has a legacy of transformation and community investment that has few rivals in Brantford. We know how significant Danny and his family have been to the Freedom House story as well.

We shared all of this with Danny on our lunch meeting leading up to giving him the Honourary Freedom Houser award. We were trying our best to honour, bless and thank him. But, all he wanted to do is thank us for affording him the opportunity of giving back to the city that he loves.

What an amazing community champion he is, coming from a legacy of community champions.

2018 HONOURARY FREEDOM HOUSER - JEN MIDDLETON

Jen Middleton is the Community Events Coordinator for the Parks and Recreation Department for the city of Brantford. We met her when she came to work with Lori-Dawn as one of her assistants.

Jen became the coordinator of Harmony Square in our downtown. That put us in a direct working relationship with her many times a year. Most of the events described in this book happen in Harmony Square including: Frosty Fest, Movies in the Square, Baptism in the Square, The Living Nativity and many others.

She seems to have an endless amount of energy and spends it consistently to make our city a better place. Like, Lori-Dawn, she goes way beyond what is necessary in her regular work hours and what anyone could expect from any one person.

Besides her work for the city, Jen is very busy in her unwavering passion of helping those in our community who need a helping hand. One of the most creative ways she does this is through her bi-annual "Pop-Up Street Store". A *Street Store* is a unique and free shopping experience for anyone in need, with the mission to provide previously enjoyed clothing, shoes and various personal items all for free.

Jen is a remarkable young lady and a joy to be around. Her passion for people and love for our city is both undeniable and admirable. She is a true community Champion.

THE KINDNESS AWARDS

In our endeavour to be kindness catalysts, we have also invented an evening that we call the "Kindness Awards". The *Kindness Awards* have been created to highlight stories of kindness in our city and honour local, kindness super-heroes. We encourage people in our city to nominate those that they are aware of who are making our city a better through intentional, ongoing lives of kindness.

The community, the winners and their friends come for an evening of food, fun and celebration of kindness. Past winners have ranged from moms and dads, local business people, city employees, community volunteers and many others. By sharing these stories, we are hoping to inspire others to acts of kindness within their family, friends, neighbourhood, community, and the city at large.

The Kindness Awards is one of our favourite events on our yearly calendar.

PARTICIPATING IN THE TRANSFORMATION OF THE CITY

No one person or organization could ever take credit for city transformation by themselves. We have found that there are many people in our city who are very passionate about having a prosperous and thriving city as well. We have come to realize that city transformation is in the heart of God and it comes out of many people, in various ways.

This chapter has been dedicated to some of the other transformation champions in our city.

When we decided to *participate in the transformation of our city,* we found many who had the same passions that we had, already there working for the same thing. For others, perhaps we have had the opportunity to be a catalyst in their community involvement.

Be committed to stepping out and getting to know other city champions in your community. You will be pleasantly surprised with the new friendships and partnerships that will be forged in the process and the ongoing momentum that will ensue as you participate in the transformation of your city.

14

A TALE OF TWO CITIES

"It was the best of times; it was the worst of times."

I have often used this line from a *Tale of Two Cities* to help those endeavouring to see sustainable transformation in their cities. Often, incredible forward progress in one area will happen, while there is significant challenge in another. For example, while you're experiencing great joy in relationships, you may be facing financial struggles. Experiencing a great victory at an event can happen while simultaneously having significant team challenges. Very rarely is life all roses or all thorns. Learning to navigate and keep momentum with these truths in front of us is necessary in the life of city transformers.

"IT WILL ONLY BE HARD IF YOU EXPECT EASE."

"It will only be hard if you expect ease."

That was what the Lord said to me coming into one of the early years of Freedom House. I had heard messages like that before. Usually it means, *buckle up your seat belt because this ride is about to get very bumpy*. And it did, for many months.

I have looked back on that word from God many times and to be honest, it has been one of the greatest things that He has ever said to me. We were never promised ease; we were promised an overcoming spirit.

Jesus said, "in this world you will have trouble, but don't be afraid because I have overcome the world."

The road of transformation is an exciting one. It is full of more fun and more favour than you ever could have imagined. It is also full of more challenges and set-backs than you would ever want to consider. Since expectations are so important as we set off in any path in life, I have added a chapter that discusses the more challenging stories along our transformation journey.

IT'S A MARATHON, NOT A SPRINT

Transformation will take *WAY LONGER* than you ever expected.

For someone who wants to have the answer before I ask the question, this was a hard one for me. I wish someone would have told me this before we started. The reality is that transformation is a *marathon and not a sprint* and this has become more and more real every passing year.

Hear God and obey...

BREAKER ANOINTING AND BRIDGES

The same year that God said, "it will only be hard if you expect ease," He had some other words of insight for us.

Every year I ask the Lord for a word or phrase to set as a theme for us at Freedom House. That year, the theme was "Breakthrough". What a great word to come into a new year with. Who wouldn't like that?

He gave me a picture to go with the word. God said, "I'm going to make you like an icebreaker, the boat that goes first and clears the way for other boats to follow. Then He got very specific and He showed me the very front of the ice-breaker, which was the front of the boat, covered in thick steel that splits the ice wide open.

"That," He said, "Is going to be how you feel at times on this path you have asked me to take you on. Breakthrough will come, but it always comes at a cost. But, it will only be hard if you expect ease."

Around the same time, God said, "I'm going to make you a bridge".

Another great invitation, right?! Who doesn't want to connect people and their destinies; or people with other people? That's what came to my mind.

Before that could sink in, the Lord continued, "I'm going to make you a bridge, and bridges get walked on. But it will only be hard if you expect ease."

Hear God and obey...

THE MOST VOCAL PEOPLE MAY BE THE LEAST RESPONSIVE PEOPLE

There were some people that were very proactive in getting us to start Freedom House.

They never showed up for anything.

Hear God and obey...

SOCIAL ACTION AND HOLY SPIRIT REVIVALISTS

Some churches are strongly justice driven. They are the ones who meet the practical needs in the city. They serve the less fortunate, bring clothing and food to those who are in need and stand up for those without a voice. They are the church involved in Social action.

Some churches are strongly Spirit driven. These are the worshippers and the intercessors, the prophetic voices and the revivalists.

Too often these groups never connect.

We believe that the *Ekklesia* is both of these groups. Holy Spirit led, socially active Christians bringing the love of God to their cities in both supernatural and natural ways.

We need to pray like it all depends on God and work like it all depends on us.

At Freedom House we choose to both pray hard and work hard.

Interestingly, we have been criticized by the social activists that we're too Holy Spirit driven and we've been labelled by the Holy Spirit crowd as being too socially minded.

Hear God and obey...

SOMETIMES NOTHING HAPPENS

I wish I could say that every time we set up for a Flippin' Friday we see miracles, or that everyone who comes to Frosty Fest immediately starts coming to Freedom House on Sundays, but that just doesn't happen.

In fact, there are some days after an event is over that I will think, what was that all about?

Sometimes all that happens from an event is that we have sown a bunch more seeds. No great stories, nothing miraculous, just more seeds.

Then, one Tuesday during staff prayer the Lord asked us if we would be willing to have enough faith to believe that every seed was eventually going to bring a harvest?

We said, "yes". This is very helpful in the days when we are walking in obedience, but it looks like nothing is happening. God assured us through this that He was always working behind the scenes and that just because we can't see it, doesn't mean it's not happening.

That helped us to stay passionate, whether we were experiencing the miraculous or the mundane.

Hear God and obey...

YOU WILL BE ACCUSED OF STUFF YOU HAVE NEVER DONE

It was a Tuesday in the middle of the summer and I thought I'd change up our Freedom House staff day a bit by taking our group to hear a well-known speaker in a nearby city.

About 2 hours into this event, one of my staff told me that I should look at our Freedom House Facebook Page. When I did, I immediately saw what he was talking about. A downtown business owner had posted a very nasty story about Freedom House on his Facebook page, which he had shared on our Facebook page and it already had a couple hundred comments and many "shares".

The business owner had a small restaurant that was struggling to survive. While I didn't agree with his perspective, he felt like our Flippin' Friday BBQs were taking business away from him and "taking food off his family's table."

We cut the casual, staff day short and headed back into town to see what we could do to take care of the growing problem. We got back into Brantford and decided that we would grab a coffee and talk through our options. During our discussion we were reminded that there was another downtown advocate who had been upset with how we were doing our Kindness Project and that we hadn't partnered with him on a specific endeavour that he was doing.

After we talked about what was happening with both of these scenarios, we prayed and asked God what we should do.

I felt like He said, "Pay two months of the businessman's rent and offer to stop running Flippin' Fridays for the rest of the summer."

I argued, "But God, we are not doing anything wrong."

Again, I heard, "Pay two months of his rent and offer to stop running Flippin' Fridays for the rest of the summer."

So, I told my staff what I had heard, we prayed together and felt like that was what God wanted us to do.

As we were getting ready to leave, I told my staff that I needed to go and do that right away before I talked myself out of it.

The truth was, we did not have two months of rent money available to pay this guy as summer months were often very lean financially for us. But, I invited Dave to come along and we quickly walked over to the restaurant to obey the Lord.

When we walked in, the restaurant was almost empty; except for the owner of the restaurant and the other gentlemen who had been challenging us about our Kindness Project. God had been very specific about what we were to do with both of these men. We were to walk up and apologize for not being more honouring of their pursuits and offer to help them.

The first man was blown away by our act of humility. He immediately apologized and said that he had over-reacted and that he was very pleased with all the stuff we were doing to make our city better. That interaction could not have gone better.

Next was the restaurant owner. I asked if I could speak with him at one of his more private tables. When we sat down, I immediately apologized for not being more aware of his needs and then I told him about how we had just come from our Freedom House staff meeting where God had directed us to pay for two months of his rent and offer to stop running Flippin' Friday for the rest of the summer.

He was shocked. He was silent for a number of seconds and then expressed his pain of not doing well in business and that he was concerned for his family, but he should not have taken it out on us. I told him that I understood his pain and his desire to be a good provider. I told him that we would get a check to him within 7 days. I prayed for him and we left the restaurant.

God had worked out the whole commotion in one visit. Before we got back to Freedom House, the restaurant owner had already posted on Facebook about our visit with him and about our generous offer to help him out. Within minutes, news got around about how this had been settled so well and God received glory from what could have been a relational disaster in our downtown.

And, to top the whole story off, he showed up in Church the next Sunday. We took an offering and received exactly what we needed to pay his 2 months of rent.

Hear God and obey...

YOU MAY GET FIRED FROM A JOB YOU NEVER WANTED; FOR DOING EXACTLY WHAT YOU WERE HIRED TO DO AND THEN ASKED TO STAY ON AT THAT SAME PLACE TO KEEP DOING WHAT YOU HAD BEEN DOING, BUT NOT OFFICIALLY ON STAFF ANYMORE.

This is probably just hypothetical (wink, wink.)

Hear God and obey...

MOLDY BREAD AND NO HEAT

Sometimes, after a *hypothetical firing*, God still tells you to stay in a city. Sometimes staying where God tells you to stay comes with no work; which means no money; which means your bills don't get paid and you don't have enough money to feed your family.

You know you're in a deep hole when you have your young family huddled around an old fireplace to keep warm because your heat and hydro have been turned off by the city because you can't pay the bills. While at the same time, God is saying stay in the city.

You know you're in a deep hole when you are given old bread to feed your family. Bread so old, that even the Food Bank doesn't want it.

Hear God and obey...

PUT EVERYTHING ON THE LINE

Sometimes banks and mortgage brokers don't always follow through on offers previously made.

Sometimes they end up expecting you to provide collateral for your new church with your own house.

No one thought this was a good idea.

Hear God and obey...

NAMES WILL NEVER HURT ME

Finally, here's a brief list of a few of the names we have been given over the years as we have served the city. Let me qualify this by assuring you that we really do have a good name in our city. Most people really like us. But some people have a different opinion.

List of some of the names we have been given through the years:

A circus who has their reward.
A group that adds to Brantford's negative image.
A freak show.
A ticking time bomb.
Bizarre.
Braggarts
Brantford's own Branch Davidians.
Cult leader.
Disgusting.
False teacher and brainwasher.
Haters.
Hypocrites.
Ignorant.
Inappropriate and misusers of public spaces.

Leading people towards needing a mental hospital.
Not real Christians whose name will be wiped from the Book of Life.
Political propagandists and sleaze bucket lobbyers.
Profiteers.
Propagandist.
Proselytizers.
Ridiculous religious ritualists.
Snake handlers.
Those who support public hangings, public circumcision, crucifixions, stonings, and burning witches at the stake.
Hear God and obey...

THE GOOD, THE BAD AND THE UGLY

It is important to know that around the time that God said "it will only be hard if you expect ease" that the revelation came to me that "you can't have a bad day with a good God."

He assured us that whatever comes our way is for our good and His glory. His word declares that every day is a day that the Lord has made that we are commanded to rejoice in it.

Ultimately, even if things happen in my day that the enemy plans for my harm, He can turn them around for my good if I allow Him to and if I choose to see with His perspective.

You can't have a bad day with a good God.

Hear God and obey...

15

MAKING YOUR CITY, THE CITY OF GOD

500 years ago, the Protestant Reformation changed the landscape of the church forever. The revelation to Martin Luther that "the just shall live by faith" became the foundation of what would bring back the salvation message to the average person and re-establish Jesus as the only way to heaven. It was a rediscovery that salvation is by God's grace alone, through faith alone, in Christ alone, to the glory of God alone. There is no doubt that this was the greatest outcome of the Reformation.

I believe, however, the second most important rediscovery from the Reformation was meant to be the *priesthood of all believers*. While it is clear that some writing comes from the Reformers regarding their disdain for the hierarchal system that had existed between the clergy and laity, a long-term solution to this challenge did not prevail. Within a few years, the newly formed Protestant churches developed the same divisions and they are prevalent even today.

But God's word is clear:

1 Peter 2:9 says, *But you are a chosen people, a royal priesthood, a holy nation, God's special possession, that you may declare the praises of him who called you out of darkness into his wonderful light.*

Transformational ecclesiology is that which acknowledges and honours all the gifts and callings within the body of Christ. No hierarchy, no sacred

/ secular divide, no callings better than the others. It is the *Ekklesia* rising up together, bringing the Kingdom of God to all the spheres of society in an integrated way, on earth as it is in heaven.

Signs of a new reformation are everywhere now. All over the world God is raising up His priesthood to function in every influential sector of our cities to bring His glorious Kingdom to earth. People are believing for God's Kingdom culture to come to their cities like never before in recorded history.

Twenty-first century reformers and transformers embrace the necessity to function as the priesthood of all believers.

CITIES OF GOD

It happened in the Bible; it happened in history; why couldn't it happen now?

Why couldn't it happen in Brantford? Why couldn't Brantford be the *city of God*?

At the beginning of our journey most people didn't believe it and many people mocked us for even considering it. To be honest, for many years it was a prophetic declaration that little or no physical evidence for us to see in the natural. But, now we are seeing the tangible outflow of what city transformation looks like.

Because of our story, people in other places in Canada are inspired and believing for their cities as well. People in the USA, Great Britain, Hong Kong, South Africa, Australia, New Zealand, Hawaii, Indonesia, Argentina – literally all over the globe, are believing for their cities to become the city of God.

What is a *city of God*?

It is a city where God is given prominence and pre-eminence; where He has Lordship and Rulership. It is where His Kingdom culture supersedes any man-made culture that has been previously established. It is where righteousness, peace, and joy so permeate the atmosphere, that everyone recognizes it and celebrates it.

It is a city where the most comfortable person, is God, Himself.

Isaiah 66:1 and 2 reads This is what the Lord says: "Heaven is my throne, and the earth is my footstool. Where is the house you will build for me? Where will my resting place be? Has not my hand made all these things, and so they came into being?" declares the Lord. "These are the ones I look on with favor: those who are humble and contrite in spirit, and who tremble at my word."

Cities will become *footstools* for the Lord to rest in, and when God finds a place where He is comfortable, the overflow of his presence will not be contained.

In those places, there will be undeniable, unmistakable, unmissable moves of God that will transform cities and nations.

GOD'S PLANS FOR OUR CITIES

Unfortunately, many people live in cities that can be described as dry and weary - cities with no hope and no future. But, this is not the will of God for our cities. He has good plans, full of hope and prosperity that He wants us to agree with and fight for until we see His vision come to pass.

We started this book by quoting a very familiar passage of scripture from *Jeremiah 29:11 "For I know the plans I have for you," declares the Lord, "plans to prosper you and not to harm you, plans to give you hope and a future."*

Do you remember who this was written to? It was written to God's people, but more specifically, it was written to God's people who were in Babylonian captivity. The Babylonians are known historically as those who became very creative in how to defeat, mistreat and humiliate those that they have conquered. It is to these people that God writes "For I know the plans I have for you," declares the Lord, "plans to prosper you and not to harm you, plans to give you hope and a future." God goes beyond just this encouragement; He gives them some practical advice on how to see this prosperity realized in *Jeremiah 29:4–7. [4]This is what the Lord Almighty, the God of Israel, says to all those I carried into exile from Jerusalem to Babylon: [5]"Build houses and settle down; plant gardens and eat what they produce. [6]Marry and have sons and daughters; find wives for your sons and give your daughters in marriage, so that they too may have sons and daughters. Increase in number there; do not decrease. [7]Also, seek the peace and prosperity of the city to which I have carried you into exile. Pray to the Lord for it, because if it prospers, you too will prosper."*

Did you see that?

Build houses and settle down;

Plant gardens and eat what they produce;
Marry and have sons and daughters;
Increase in number there; do not decrease.

Settle down, settle in, settle on the fact that God wants to bring transformation to your city.

Is God working in our city? Is God working in our schools? Is God working in our government? Is God working in our businesses? Is God at work on our streets?

Here's the great news: the answer to these questions is "yes." God is *ALREADY* at work in your city.

In the next few years entire cities will come to Jesus. The buildings will not be big enough to hold what Jesus will do in those cities. God is presently preparing the church to love and serve and be ready for this to happen. God wants your city to be one of those cities.

Therefore, pray for your city. Bless your city. Bring peace and prosperity to your city.

Partner with Holy Spirit to make your city, the *City of God*.

NOTES

2. THE VISION FOR CITIES

1. Hebrews 12:1
2. https://www.rottentomatoes.com/m/silent_hill/
3. Used with permission. To discover the circumstances around the writing of this poem, and its extraordinary global impact, check out the book Red Moon Rising by Pete Greig (David C. Cook). You can watch The Vision film at www.24-7prayer.com/thevisionfilm

3. THREE STRIKES AND YOU'RE...?

1. Fun Fact: *The Book,* we found out 15 years later that the person who sent that book to Ghana did so, by revelation from God himself. Jesica MacNaughton (nee:Silvoso) was in charge of where her father's books were to be sent, as part of the family ministry. She remembers very distinctly sending ONE COPY of *That None Should Perish* to an obscure Christian book store in Ghana, West Africa in 2000. It was that very book that Dave found and read while serving as a missionary there.

4. THE CITY OF GOD

1. https://www.britannica.com/topic/The-city-of-God
2. Romans 4:17
3. I first heard the term Polipneumaclimatologist from Jon Peterson who at the time was a leader in 24-7 Prayer USA.
4. Dr. Ed Silvoso, *Prayer Evangelism* (Ventura California; Regal Books, 2000) p.88
5. Dr. Ed Silvoso, *Transformation* (Ventura California: Regal Books, 2007) p. 28,29
6. Dr. Ed Silvoso, Transformation (Ventura California: Regal Books, 2007) p. 117
7. J. H. Thayer, *A Greek-English Lexicon of the New Testament* (Peabody, Massachusetts: Hendrickson Publishers) p. 196; and Oskar Seyffert, *A Dictionary of Classical Antiquities* (New York, New York: MacMillan and Company) p. 202–203.
8. I highly recommend the book *Ekklesia*, by Dr. Ed Silvoso for in-depth understanding on this topic. (Ada Michigan; Baker Publishing Group)

6. HEAR GOD AND OBEY

1. God speaks in many ways; through His word, thoughts, impressions, dreams & visions, it is not always audible. It is the responsibility of every child of God to discern the voice of the Father for themselves.
2. Script transcribed from YouTube clip of Seinfeld show.

NOTES

7. FREEDOM HOUSE - A MINISTRY CENTRE WHERE CHURCH HAPPENS

1. Dr. Ed Silvoso, *Prayer Evangelism* (Ventura California: Regal Books, 2000) p.88

10. THE GOSPEL OF THE KINGDOM

1. **Strong's #4982:** sozo (pronounced sode'-zo) from a primary sos (contraction for obsolete saos, "safe"); to save, i.e. deliver or protect (literally or figuratively):--heal, preserve, save (self), do well, be (make) whole.
2. Dr. Ed Silvoso *Transformation* (Ventura California; Regal Books, 2007) p. 132
3. Dr. Myles Munroe, *Rediscovering the Kingdom* (Shippensburg, PA: Destiny Image Publishers 2004) p. 54
4. Bill Johnson, *When Heaven Invades Earth* (Shippensburg, PA: Destiny Image Publishers, 2010) p. 12
5. http://www.marketplaceleaders.org/the-gospel-of-the-kingdom
6. Chuck Colson, *How Now Shall We Live*, (Wheaton Illinois: Tyndale House Publishers, 1999) p. 7
7. Loren Cunningham, *Making Jesus Lord* (Seattle Washington: YWAM Publishing, 1998) p. 58
8. Pete Greig, *Red Moon Rising* (Colorado Springs, Colorado: David C. Cook, 2015) p. 144
9. Deuteronomy 8:18
10. Bill Bright, *My Life is Not My Own* (Ventura California: Regal Books, 2010) p. 112
11. Dick Staub, *The Culturally Savvy Christian* (San Francisco, California: Jossey-Bass Imprint, 2007) p. 29
12. Romans 14:17
13. "https://www.seedbed.com/church-business-or-Kingdom-business/" *by Howard Snyder*
14. Loren Cunningham, *Winning God's Way* (Seattle, Washington: YWAM Publishing, 1989) p.132

11. THE CULTURE OF THE KINGDOM

1. Source: dictionary.com

CITY of GOD

Transformed People, Transforming Cities

Brian Beattie Ph.D.

APPENDIX

HOW TO TRANSFORM A CITY

The following is a timeline that will help with expectations and momentum for those desiring to see God bring His Kingdom in their city as it is in heaven. City transformation has both predictable and progressive aspects that will give practitioners reasonable points of celebration and future planning.

This is a high-level outline for quick reference. We are presently developing this in more detail for both church and marketplace contexts. This outline is not a perfect pattern, but, if you're serious about the time, resource and efforts that it will take for city transformation, this appendix will be the most referenced part of the book.

1 - DREAM

God has a dream for your city that His Kingdom would come in all its fullness. This dream is wrapped up in Jesus' statement that he made when He said He would build his church – EKKLESIA. The dreaming stage usually starts by hearing other stories (Biblical, historical or current) of what God has done or is doing in other cities.

Paul's statement "faith comes by hearing" in Romans 10 is not just reserved for hearing to the point of salvation alone, but also to believe God for the blessing of inheritance for all those who live a life of obedience.

Can you dream with God for your city and beyond?

2 - EMBRACE PERSONAL RENEWAL

God will be continually working on you and your character as your partner with him in transformation, and that's ok. Become a worshipper and learn to enjoy intimacy with God. Learn to *hear God and obey* for yourself. Learn to *hear God and obey* with your spouse. Learn to *hear God and obey* as a family.

Personal transformation is mandatory in the pursuit of city transformation.

Transformed people transform cities.

What does transformation mean to me?

What will it cost?

How do I need to think, act and live differently?

3 - ENGAGE YOUR IMMEDIATE SPHERE OF INFLUENCE - CHURCH AND MARKETPLACE

Inspire, engage and teach your staff, your leadership or your co-workers. Teach them that God is working in all the spheres of influence and that genuine transformation can't come unless He does (no division of sacred/secular.)

Find your *cohesive core* (like-minded leaders) and start with them. In any group 5% will be visionaries; 15% will be implementers; and 80% will be managers. Your *cohesive core* will consist of the visionaries and the implementers.

Worship and pray together to change the spiritual atmosphere around your church/business. Hear God and Obey.

Who are your cohesive core?

What are some early wins? (Some examples would be: clean a park, $1 Car Wash, community BBQ, etc.).

4 - BUILD CITY-WIDE CHURCH UNITY

Build a city-wide Transformation Team (e.g. ONEchurch/ Community Action Team). A transformation team is the city-wide *Ekklesia* coming together to solve challenges in the city which includes both church and marketplace ministers.

Carefully build relational, philosophical and functional unity in a city-wide manner. As with point 3, look for your city-wide cohesive core.

Agree on the mission of your group. (e.g. "ONECHURCH - participating in the transformation of the city.")

Is there an existing Pastors' Network/Transformation Network in your city? How do we bless it? If there is not, should we start one?

Who is your cohesive core?

How will you build unity?

What are some easy wins together? (Adopt a Street prayer, Joint service, clean a park, Civic Prayer Breakfast, etc.)

5 - EVALUATE THE NEEDS OF THE CITY

The city knows what it needs - ASK – this will establish relationships and intent. The church exists in the city to serve not to be served. Make sure you are willing to work before you ask.

ILLUSTRATION: We are going to build a NET under our cities - (no holes where people are missed & no clumps where too much time and resource are being spent on the same issues)

Address mindsets about systemic poverty (Material, Motivational, Relational and Spiritual.)

What are the needs of the City? (homelessness, jobs, economy, families, etc.)

6 - BUILD STRATEGIC COMMUNITY RELATIONSHIPS

Build external relationships with other city leaders from a variety of spheres both Christian & non-Christian.

Step into relational circles and begin to meet needs with no-strings attached.

Consider starting a Civic Prayer Breakfast to bless civic leaders like the Mayor, Counsellors, and First Responders. (This is not an opportunity to ask for what you need or want.)

Who are the other solution oriented people or groups in your city?

What can you export to other cities or regions from what you have learned so far?

7 - SERVE TOGETHER STRATEGICALLY & CONSISTENTLY

Intentionally target needs from your analysis of the city in #5. Be sure to address the *felt needs* first. Include marketplace people in serving, releasing ministers in all spheres to serve where they are.

Address roots of issues in your city. Include both food and clothing initiatives, as well as job and wealth creation opportunities.

What does it look like when God's Kingdom comes "on earth as is it is heaven?"

How do we address the root issues of material, motivational, relational and spiritual challenges?

8 - ESTABLISH PROSPEROUS CULTURAL NORMS

By now, the *CHURCH / Ekklesia* is seen as an active partner in the city and welcomed as normal. We have a proven track record of bringing positive solutions to real needs in our cities.

Righteousness, peace and joy are normal in the Kingdom of God. Are they normal in your city?

How is the Church perceived in your city?

Are we solution oriented?

Are we givers or takers?

9 - CREATE PERMANENT PLACES OF BLESSING

Create community hubs that are resource centres for material, motivational, relational and spiritual prosperity (Dream Centre model).

Create a FOUNDATION where people apply for grants that are meeting needs in the city.

Start wealth creating businesses.

Establish Schools of Transformation: training centres for ongoing education and application.

Start a 24/7 Worship & Prayer Centre for continual worship and prayer over your city.

Do you have a long-term plan of how to perpetuate blessing in your city?

What people or groups have the vision and capacity to be these Hubs or Blessings Centres?

10 - DREAM BIGGER

The city isn't transformed until everyone is living prosperous lives - Material, Motivational, Relational, Spiritual.

Incorporate long term, multi-generational thinking and planning.

What's the next step in your city?

What other cities are you called to influence? Start looking regionally or even nationally, asking God for His guidance.

FREEDOM ENCOUNTER

We have found that too many Christians are living "*saved, but not free*". We're convinced this is not God's will for our lives. God wants us to live free, victorious lives... now!

We can say this with confidence because we have experienced it and we have seen God do this over and over again for those who have participated in a Freedom Encounter weekend.

Freedom Encounter is a series of 6 teachings that walk Christians into Biblical truths of what the Bible says about God and what the Bible says about us. When we have a healthy God-image, and a healthy self-image we can truly live out of the great commandment which says "Love the Lord your God with all your heart, soul, mind and strength and love your neighbour, as yourself." (Luke 10:27)

We have seen God walk many, many people into a life of Freedom and we know that this is His design for you as well.

There are six sessions provided in the Facilitator and Student workbooks; plus a 21 day devotional – 21 Days of Freedom. For more info email brian@freedomhouse.ca.

FREEDOM
ENCOUNTER
21 Day Devotio
FREEDOM
ENCOUNTER
21 Day Devotional
Brian Beattie Ph.D.
Sharlyss Beattie Ph.D.

SUPERHERO IN ME PROMO.

THE KINDNESS PROJECT

The Kindness Project is all about changing cities BY good INTO good through multi-level, coordinated, intentional, strategic KINDNESS. The Kindness Project explores the untapped level of synergy and interconnectedness between business, government, social agencies, the church, education and the people of a community. The Kindness Project facilitates transformation on both a neighbourhood and city-wide scale: resulting in ordinary people recreating the culture through a lifestyle of kindness.

Over the years, we've run Kindness Campaign's where we canvass neighbourhoods and ask if people will be kind to their neighbours. We've done 1$ Car Washes where we GIVE people a dollar for the honour of serving them. We've done free barbecues in dangerous neighbourhoods until 2am to create a "bubble of kindness" when people need it.

For more information visit www.thekindnessproject.ca

THE KINDNESS PROJECT

To order more copies of this book or for additional resources visit www.brianbeattie.ca

Ekkle-sia later!

Printed in Great Britain
by Amazon